Life Planning

How to make a plan for your own future for your own life

YOUNG BAMBOO

authorHOUSE®

AuthorHouse™ UK Ltd.
500 Avebury Boulevard
Central Milton Keynes, MK9 2BE
www.authorhouse.co.uk
Phone: 08001974150

First published by AuthorHouse 3/19/2010

ISBN: 978-1-4490-8605-3 (sc)

This book is printed on acid-free paper.

CONTENTS

INTRODUCTION

A successful life deals with the relationship between the activities and its goals. This is clearly an extremely difficult process, because all lives are dynamic, complex and unpredictable. Globalisation, technology, knowledge and the ever-changing way of life has a general impact overall on people's performance. Therefore, knowing your own life and capabilities determine its effects on performing those processes at a dynamic level, using your own abilities. It is however, most useful for you to focus on having a dynamic life using your own capabilities, and how these can be developed on an ongoing basis.

Today virtually all people should be considering making life plans. In those plans are your primary resources and source of uniqueness. This must obviously be the true reality of people's lives. Clearly, the primary resources of life planning are coming from your own dreams, goals, strategies and life experience. The truth is that life planning can be developed purposefully in order to understand the nature and value of the intangible assets, which are the foundations of planning your life based on your dreams.

In fact, life planning and life management techniques are the most important tools to success. Planning is preparing a sequence of action points to achieve some specific goal. This planning will help you to do it effectively, and can help you reduce much of the necessary time and effort in achieving that life goal. The author attempts to critically identify whether your life strategy is balanced with your talents and abilities, which can result in you succeeding in your life.

Planning is in fact like a map. When following a plan you can always see how much you have progressed towards your projected goal and how far you are from your destination. Knowing where you are is essential for making good decisions on where to go or what to do next.

Life planning can serve the needs of your own life, build your reputation, improve your quality of life and enhance both your short and long term life. Life plans are concerned with privacy and confidentiality in all of your life interactions, because people's lives are all complex.

This planning focuses on the very changes which life can bring, and enables you to deal with life's problems more effectively. Today planning for life should be undertaken because life is difficult. The benefits of planning are now more widely dispersed throughout people's lives than ever before. No, planning is not a life or death situation but it can be beneficial in working through life's difficulties.

You should plan "long-term" because the time span of plans is essential to your purpose or to your process of planning. However, there are many principles you should apply to your planning for each division of your life, as much as having a plan for your life, as a whole. Strategic planning can put some people off, including some of those constructively engaged in strategic planning. Strategic planning is the main focus of this article, this involves; thought, assessments, estimations, and judgments leading to choices made today about where your life should go from here, and how to get there.

The purpose of planning is always aimed at reducing risks. Today, most people realise that the most hazardous form of speculation is to not speculate and so, the main characteristic of today's planning is to make assumptions, assessments, guesses and evaluations from the past, and for the present and the future.

Planning is difficult especially when it concerns the future. The greater the degree of uncertainty about the future, the greater the need to plan. A plan sets out the intentions for yourself for your life after careful thought. The truth is the future of your life is uncertain, which is a good reason why you should have a plan. (Martin, 2007).

Life planning is a guided process by which one takes stock of one's life, helping to clarify dreams, goals, talents, and challenges, and identifies the steps necessary to create the life one wants to live. Life planning addresses many dimensions of life (these depend on your own circumstances, you can change or adapt them for your own aims), the author has included the following:

1. Health
2. Education
3. Work and Career
4. Finances
5. Skills
6. Family Relationships
7. Spiritual or Religious Life
8. Social Life and Friends
9. Assets
10. Life Style or Freedom

The areas mentioned above are the most important basics in everyone's lives. Life planning ensures that you envision the life you want, make specific plans, address the issues that need resolution and have the resources to fully live and enjoy the life you have envisioned.

There are many books or websites that can assist you to establish your life planning, but these are normally just in the short term. For example, they may help you to set out a five year plan but this book will help you to make a plan for your whole life. This book will guide you through many life stages, developing practical plans to help you achieve each goal for your whole life.

This also includes a life-line; this will help you to decrease the confusion which very often happens to everyone undergoing a major life transition. The author has used his life experiences (more than 30 years) both compassionate and passionate about helping people clarify their life talents and goals, finding purpose and meaning in their lives. Using practical tables, assessments and several life planning tools, the author will provide support and guidance to help you to gain clarity, move through your transition and step into this next phase of your life with confidence.

The author's background includes years of work in human development, sales, business and management, as well as 25 years in global corporation companies such as Holiday Inn, Accor Hotels Group, Radisson, and Financial Industry. The author has initiated programmes not specific to anyone and has developed life planning as a life tool for you to retain. This may range from finding new talents and goals to help start or begin planning your life, completing a practical table, establishing your life goals or transferring your goals to your life plan as a life tool.

The life planning programme helps you to develop alternatives to be able to measure your own life in terms of how successful you are in many different stages, from an initial career building age to approaches to life and career planning for extended middle age. The plan will help to motivate you to stay focused on your career to success, enabling you to stay on your plan until retirement and finally to the end of your life. The author has developed the programme using the talents you already have, putting them in place, transferring them to your current role, then assessing strengths and interests, exploring options and building balanced "portfolios", creating life strategies and activities which drive you to work harder than ever.

Working differently is a sign of personal achievement and professional career planning which implements a custom tailored portfolio of career opportunities, which allow for greater flexibility and personal satisfaction. Creating this programme can help you organise your personal life, finances, work, and family relationship needs. In addition, this book works with academic, corporate and private sector, helping you to design your own lifestyle that results in your personal life changing dramatically.

This book creates rich and balanced lives of engagement, purpose and passion, using the personal imagination as a tool for developing a vision and choosing goals that will drive you to the next stage of your life. It guides you to make specific plans, setting priorities and timetables. It will continue to work with you to stay on track and maintain momentum as you move to create the life you want to live. With 25 years of experience working and coaching people in transition, the author has worked with people re-directing careers, following corporate downsizing, individuals initiating career change or exploring life options, and those seeking a different balance between work and the rest of their life.

This book navigates change and processes for you to bring creative thought, reflection and personal planning to different ages of life transition. The author believes that thoughtful attention to decision-making can result in endless life possibilities, influencing you and even generations to come. This book is going to help you to re-design your life style and career change and life success. It is particular passionate for bringing intention and vision to the development of personal legacies.

This book also provides executive and leadership coaching, career management consulting and coaching services for you at all stages in everyone' lives and careers. It focuses on guiding you through a process which helps you recognise the value and uniqueness, define your "top of the mountain" and find satisfaction in your work and private life. The author's passion is derived from helping people from any background, rich, poor, or popular, to think creatively, explore and embrace new possibilities, make connections and achieve your goals and finally your life. It will also help you to clarify where you want to go, and help you to get there.

The author is passionate about the importance of life having growth, meaning and enjoyment in every stage. It also helps you change the "crises" of life transitions into exciting opportunities and "adventure" with a focus of building on your talent and strength. The author is especially interested in life balance for caregivers, creating a new life for yourself and for retirement, and helping you pro-actively design your own future.

It can enable you to improve your personal life qualities, creativity, big-picture perspective, practicality, and finally help you to become a warmer and kinder person. It brings exciting changes and development with a greater understanding of human nature, of life, of what really matters, in different areas and ways of being, such as:

- An increased individuality and authenticity, a freedom to be who you are
- An increase in creativity and in spirituality, a search for purpose
- An increase in civic engagement in giving your time, in helping society, in mentoring others
- A new imperative to conserve and pass on your values and stories to other generations.

In fact, this is potentially the time of your life where you have more choice, perspective and wisdom to make a meaningful impact on your world. With a clear vision and plan for your whole life, you can improve your finances, education, assets, family relationships, spirituality, friends, and needs for the life you plan to create.

Life planning will help you indentify your values, passions, gifts and dreams, decide who you are and what you want to do and be in this world. With this knowledge, your life planning can guide you to develop visions, goals, talents and plans for your future.

This book is suitable for everyone who is ambitious, hungry, and ready to progress as quickly as possible and to start succeeding in life. This book has been written for anyone who is passionate about his or her future life. The ideas, and any techniques in this book will help you to achieve your goal, both short term and long-term, and for your whole life. Finally, it will help you to succeed faster than you ever thought possible.

This book is also a tool for life, in other words, it is a bible for life which could be used to help you predict your whole life future. Clearly, this could enable you to see exactly what you are going to be in both the near and distant future. This book is a strong light, helping someone who does not want to walk in the dark anymore. The reality is we all are living in a dark world, if you don't know what you want to be, if you have no goal of what you want to achieve, if you have nothing important in your life, or your aims or goals which you want to achieve are not clear enough, then something might be trying to tell you that you are walking in the dark.

Therefore, this book is obviously suitable for you. This book is going to concentrate on only you specifically not someone else. Why? Because you are the most important person in your life, how simple is that? However, this book is something of a guiding light which everyone's lives need, as the author mentioned earlier that we all are living in a dark world, where we cannot tell where we are. Unfortunately, it is also a dangerous world, where people are fighting, killing, and destroying. So what you really need is a light, whatever kind of light it is but you still need some kind of light, it could be a candle, electric light, or any kind of light - it depends on what kind of light you are looking for.

However, as long as you have got some light in your life, then at least you have something to help you so that you are not walking in the dark for your whole life. You probably argue that no, you do not need the light - you feel very secure because you have got a mother, father, sister, brother, lover, son or daughter who is apparently able to protect you from the danger, who acts as a lifeguard to be able to protect you every minute of your life.

The truth is that there is no one who can be with you every day for the rest of your life, you might have some good friends and family members but there are no guarantees that they will be around forever. We all are taking risks in our lives, risks when we eat food, when we walk somewhere that is unfamiliar, sleeping somewhere that might not be safe enough. The fact is, we can all go (die) at any minute, no one really knows when. We all have to walk our paths in our individual way, our ways are all different. No matter where you are, what language you speak, how much you earn, who your parents are, what your nationality is, or where you come from, as long as you are alive, the truth is we are all different. Why is this? Because we all are human.

This book will help you to search your dreams and talents, helping you to establish and set goals for yourself, move your dreams through the process of your own life plans, the practical goal test, based on guidance which will help you to know yourself more, knowing your life and goals, and more importantly helping you to apply those talents, resulting in helping you to focus on one goal and strategy that is truly your destination.

This is a career and life plan using a special way of brainstorming, clearly focusing on your own career and whole life. This is a personal life plan which helps you to create your goals for areas like relationships, interests, giving back to community, spirituality, and other areas. In fact, it would help to build an individual population in a country, and would finally help world success, becoming a much better place to live in for all human beings.

However, once you have achieved your goal then this book is also going to help you to create a daily 'to do' list of things, that you can schedule to do today, in order for you to work towards your life time goals. At an early stage, goals may be to read books and gather information on the achievement of your goal and this will help you to improve the quality and realism of your goal setting. Finally, review your plans, and make sure that they fit in with the way in which you want to live your life.

This book has been written from both theories of science and real experience, which took time. More than 20 years has been spent on research and completed by the author's real life, where the author has been using it and practicing it, since he was 16 years old. At whatever age you are now, this book is a tool for life to help you to destroy your confusion and uncertainty, and more importantly, it is an excellent and most valuable weapon which cannot be valued in monetary terms, only by the success of your own life. In fact, this is a tool to help you to avoid risks and is the best tool to help you to be whatever you want to be and to help you to have whatever you want to have. Finally, it is to help you to see the value of your own life using appropriate methods.

These methods and processes have been fully developed as life planning which will be able to help you succeed at a higher level and in a far bigger way. The question is why not apply the same strategy to your own life? The author makes it easy to adapt this book for your own life plan and there are some practical tests to help you to adapt your life using this life tool. For example, to help you to discover your goals and strategies, task lists form every part of your life. This book is easy to follow, helping you to create goals, strategies and tasks taking you through the process to a finished whole life plan.

There are financial planning tools and career planning tools there to help you to set up your own career, using goals based on your own character guiding your talents in each area of your life. Finally, the tools help you to create expectation of achieving assets on your list, allowing you to build a life confidence which will show in every single step on your way and last you a life time.

The author suggests that you should read and repeat this book, especially the part of your own life plan. Every day, week, and month, and every single minute of your life, you should take it with you everywhere. This is an adventure for you to take advantage of in your own life, a life of unlimited imagination.

The author very sincerely hopes to see you becoming one of the top world class successes perhaps in the next five, ten or 15 years or for whenever you have planned it. The author is hoping that you will be able to achieve your goals, your plan and your dreams. Remember, it does not matter who you are, what you are, what language you speak, which nationality, colour or ethnicity you are, as long as you are alive.

This book is suitable for you if you are ambitious, hungry, looking for a better way of life, looking for a chance to improve your own life, looking to get rich or richer, looking to be a famous name, or looking to achieve with the biggest and best in the world. You will find this book is useful and directed towards your needs, and it will help you to recover your own life.

This is your book and personal journey that you can use throughout your whole life, in order to help you to achieve at a higher level; here are some steps you might have to follow starting out, based on what has worked for you. You can certainly use this book alone, without your providers and peers. However, the author would like to suggest that it would be better for you to have someone to talk to when you have decided on a goal you want to achieve, whether or not you feel things are or are not going as planned. Once you complete your task, no matter how big it is, you should plan to do something nice for yourself. The best way to stay motivated is to reward yourself along the way.

Congratulations in advance, you have the first step to making the most important change of making a life plan. Be sure to work hard, stay focused, motivate yourself and keep trying and working to get whatever you want. Re-reading this book will help you to keep your energies focused on your current goal, to achieve one by one, step by step, finally helping you to gain bigger achievements than ever before in your life. Now is the time to enjoy the adventure of your own life.

Good luck..........

Chapter 1:

The Meaning of Life and Discovering Who You Are

What is Life?

Looking for the meaning of life is not easy to describe. This is probably the best place to begin the discussion of the Earth's biogeography and to answer the following question. What is life? While the reply to this question may appear simple, scientists have actually spent considerable time pondering this problem. In fact, many scientists would suggest that humans still do not have a clear definitive answer to this question. Part of this problem is related to the existence of viruses and other forms of microscopic entities. Some scientists define viruses as very complex organic molecules, while others suggest they are the simplest form of life. Daniel (2002) suggests that something could be considered "alive" if it meets the following seven conditions:

1. Living things must have a programme to make copies of themselves from generation to generation.
2. Life adapts and evolves in step with external changes in the environment.
3. Organisms tend to be complex, highly organised, and most importantly have compartmentalised structures. Chemicals found within their bodies are synthesised through metabolic processes into structures that have specific purposes. Cells and their various organelles are examples of such structures. Cells are also the basic functioning unit of life. In multi-cellular organisms, cells are often organised into organs to create higher levels of complexity and function.
4. Living things have the ability to take energy from their environment and change it from one form to another. This energy is usually used to facilitate their growth and reproduction. People call the process that allows for this facilitation metabolism.
5. Organisms have regeneration systems that replace parts of themselves that are subject to wear and tear. This regeneration can be partial or it can involve the complete replacement of the organism. Complete replacement is necessary because partial replacements cannot stop the unavoidable decline in the functioning state of the entire living system over time. In other words, all organisms degrade into a final non-functioning state, people call death.
6. Living creatures respond to environmental stimuli through feedback mechanisms. Cues from the environment can cause organisms to react through behaviour, metabolism and physiological change. Further, responses to stimuli generally act to increase a creature's chance for day-to-day survival.

7. Organisms are able to maintain numerous metabolic reactions even in a single instance in time. Living things also keep each of these reactions separated from each other.

In summary, life is a characteristic state or mode of living, which people now call; "social life", "city life" and "real life", in fact it is the experience of being alive. It is the likely course of human events and activities. These people could no longer cope with the complexities of life, the course of the existence of an individual. The actions and events that occur in life depend on many issues; the period during which something is functional (as between birth and death) and people's lives as long as they have a happy life.

It is not that simple to describe what the meaning of life is, or to identify where a life comes from, even the biologists (people who study life) have a tough time describing what life is. But finally, the biologists have determined that all living things, do share something in common; living things which need to take in energy, get rid of waste, grow and develop, respond to the environment, reproduce and pass their traits onto their offspring and evolve (change slowly) in response to their environment. In conclusion, in order for something to be considered to "have a life" as you know it, it must possess these characteristics.

The meaning of life constitutes a philosophical question concerning the purpose and significance of human existence. This question can be expressed through a variety of related questions. For example, why you are here? What is life all about? And what is the meaning of your life? It has been a subject of much philosophical, scientific and theological speculation throughout history. There have been a large number of answers to these questions from many different cultural and ideological backgrounds.

However, there are many scientists trying to describe the meaning of life. For example, Albert (2006) describes it as "Humans are creatures spending their lives trying to convince their lives that their existing is not absurd." In fact, the meaning of life is deeply mixed with the philosophical and religious conceptions of existence, consciousness and happiness. It also touches on many other issues, such as symbolic meaning, ontology, value, purpose, ethics, good and evil, free will, conception and existence of god, the soul and the afterlife. Scientific contributions are more indirect by describing the empirical facts about the universe, science provides some contextual topics.

The author argues that the human is central, and not cosmic. The religious approach asks the question "What is the meaning of my life?" The value of their question pertaining to the purpose of life maybe considered to be confident with the achievement of ultimate reality, if that is believed by one to exist. Purpose is the cognitive awareness in cause and affects linking for achieving a goal in a given system, whether human or machine. In the most general sense, it is the anticipated result which guides decision making and in choosing appropriate actions within a range of strategies in the process (a conceptual scheme), based on varying degrees of ambiguity about the knowledge that creates the contextual nature for the action.

In brief, it can be concluded that according to the state of conditions in a given environment, usually due to a perceived better set of conditions or parameters from the previous state. This change is the motivation which may serve the focus of control and goal orientation. In psychology, the experience of lacking in purpose in one's life is known as acidity. In conclusion, the meaning of life depends on the purpose of what you are alive for, this should be helping you to answer these following questions:

Why are you here in this world? What is your life for? In fact, the goal is for you to be alive in the real world.

Who am I? Who are you?

Perhaps this is only question life really throws at you. Maybe all your specific endeavours are one way or another, directed at it. **However, now is the time to look at the definition of what your life is.** It is however, not easy for most people to understand the meaning of their own life. The most important thing is how you are going to implement yourself into your life, describing who you are then possibly; you will know the purpose of your life. To do this, you should be able to answer these following questions:

What is life? You might consider this when answering the following questions;

- Why you are alive?
- What makes you stay alive?
- What is your life for?
- What makes you most happy in your life?
- Who are you alive for?

Maybe now is the right time for you to ask yourself, try to understand yourself, in the origin of the universe, biologists working on evolution or psychologists have driven you to have the desire to find out who you are and what you are. Perhaps now take your time to think carefully. You might be driven to ask when you are lying in the bath, travelling on an extraordinary plane and living life, the question requires the same commitment and principle.

Finding out who you are, sounds too strange to be true. Now take a look at yourself in a mirror, and see that person there, how can you describe yourself? What do you see in the mirror? What do you look like? First, let's take a few minutes to go through exactly how you should be answering these questions, using the following questions below as a guide.

1. Who am I?
2. Where do I come from? Who are my parents?
3. Am I a daughter (a son, a brother, a sister, a mother, a father, an uncle, an aunt, a friend) or someone else?
4. Am I living healthily?
5. Am I getting a good enough education?
6. Am I a good worker and will I have a good career from today until I am 65?
7. Am I saving enough money from today until I am 65?
8. Are my life skills good enough to keep me alive?
9. Do I respect religion? What religion am I? What should I do to show my respect for the spiritual or religious life?
10. Am I happy to live alone? What am I supposed to do to maintain relationships with people?
11. Do I own assets of value? Do I want to have some assets?

12. Am I happy with my life style now? What life style do I have now and what will I want in the future?
13. What kind of life am I going to have before I retire and after I retire?

Those questions might help you to clarify or describe your own life. Knowing yourself is one of the most important issues. Clearly, this can help you see what you are and if you have the capacity of really living life. These questions will direct you where to go, what to do, how you are going to do it and when you are going to achieve these goals in your life. However, there are more details further on, including exercises which will help you to have a better understanding and help you to clarify your own life in the next chapter.

To find out who you really are is quite stressful and emotional. It can be complex and complicated, looking at the variety of alternatives for the way of living. There are synaptic changes that may relate to behavioural alternations. To not know yourself has the common outcome of you pleasing yourself and leading a wayward life. This is a pathetic way of living that relates to the loving and caring you, but puts you in a very untenable position in life; you are old enough to chart your life separately from others but you are allowing yourself to live in a world of loss, emptiness and uncertainty.

Consider, however, a life fully attended to and cared for by yourself; who makes a point of spending quality time on looking after yourself, growing and developing and meeting your own needs. You should be yourself all of the time, think, walk, eat, sleep, travel and mentor yourself on essential values of life. Listen to what you say, guide yourself in what you do, introduce yourself to friends, relatives and society, and have a plan for yourself and the entire family. In this exciting new life which includes your family, it is not an exaggerated thought to anticipate the development of yourself in your life as a hopeful, competitive, productive and well balanced person, always aware of duties and obligations to yourself, to your family, and to society.

Quite clearly, you could re-think being yourself using this incredible thought: your character is usually a reflection of your own family life. It tells you how you were reared by your parents and recognised by your family. If you have never had this thought, very likely, you will have a hard time knowing who you are and where you want to be.

It may be a sweeping statement, but it makes a very important point. The quality of life that you have affects the development of your individuality, and for that matter, the clarity and meaning of your future. Life Stability has so many different meanings when it comes to talking about your own life.

Stability of life doesn't necessarily mean being a wealthy person. You need to have a plan that can be followed at any age. Certain things that are done every day around the same time can be very important. It will help you develop a life that you can follow every day.

Many people are confused when it comes to having a successful family life, including being a husband or wife and with the process of parenting. The author would like to advise all readers that this is common to most people, whoever you are, whatever age you are, or what career you pursue. There is always a way, steps, or strategies that can be followed, to plan and earn success in love, life, work or marriage. In fact, these strategies are precise and easy to follow. You will be able to achieve all of the goals you want in your life. So wake up and feel active and ready to understand the successful life journey.

Chapter 2:

Identify Your Dream and Make it Come True

The Dream

Identify what you want to achieve in your life. This is a very crucial step as it will determine every decision and action that you are going to take in the future. If you don't know what you want in your life, you will be just like a lost sheep, you don't have a clear direction of where you are heading. So find out what you really want in your life before you move on.

Next, we will move on and look at your dream. A dream is a series of mental images and emotions occurring during sleep. The word "dream" Brian (2001) suggests that there are four interrelated meanings that follow one from another and when you put them together, you know what you dream is.

Firstly, a dream is a form of thinking that occurs when there is a certain, as yet undetermined minimal level of brain activation, and external stimuli are blocked from entry into the mind. People call this the "self system." This may seem overly complicated but it is worded this way because people not only dream during sleep, but also on some occasions in very relaxed waking states when people just "drift off".

Secondly, a dream is something people "experience." The imagination can make it seem very real and it can make the senses heightened, especially seeing and hearing. Usually, people are the main actor in their dream, and a dream is sometimes, though not always, very emotional.

Thirdly, a dream is what people remember in the morning, so it is a memory of the dreaming experience. Lastly, a dream can also be spoken or written about, giving a report to others about that experience, which is the only way anyone else can ever know about another person's dream. This is because they cannot be there, see it, or be told about it by the person, while it is actually happening.

In short, a dream is a report of memory of a cognitive experience that happens under the kinds of conditions that are most frequently produced in a state called "sleep". However, if you want it to be simpler, you can think of a dream as the little dreams our minds make up when the "self" system is not keeping you alert to the world around you. Most people over the age of 10 dreams at least four to six times per night during a stage of sleep called REM (Rapid Eye Movement), Chris (2002).

A distinguishing characteristic of this stage of sleep, people can sometimes have dreamlike moments during waking, if they are in a relaxed state of mind and not noticing anything in their surroundings. In summary, people can dream in REM or Non-REM sleep and perhaps even during waking, but people can also have REM sleep without dreaming. Dreams are also influenced by fears or stress which often express your current concerns and preoccupations which is called "the continuity hypothesis." If you are nervous about studying for finals, you may have nervous dreams on the same topic.

Dreams are not always negative preoccupations. For example, if you bump into someone, it is likely that you will dream about him or her. Dreams are something so forgettable, according to Chris Widener (2002) that all of us forget 95% to 99% of our dreams for the simple reason that you sleep right through them and are not paying attention to remembering anything. Therefore, with this reason in mind, it is not unusual that you would not remember or take them into account enough for them to bother you. This shows that you are not paying attention to what you are dreaming.

The most important and biggest difference is that the people who have a great interest in dreams have therefore a greater motivation to pay attention to them. At this point, your dream to become or to have something is likely to already be in your imagination, of what you would like to be or to have in your life. For some reason, these people have decided that their dreams are worth remembering so this might interest and motivate you to think that dreams are important. Moreover, some people take seriously that in a specific part of the brain it has been known that there is a way to improve their ability to dream for a period of time. You probably remember when you were young you might have had more dreams than now, and it is possible that they can predict the future (David, 1999).

Barrett (1988) also comments that dreams are creative and plausible in time, and it showed that dreams are a psychological phenomenon that has meaning in your future life. In fact, a dream is a basic truth you must accept and believe if you are to achieve your dream. Your dream can be 'reality' which is a way to guide you through to your future, so you can actually see yourself living your dream.

Chris (2002) suggests a dream can be a reality if it is not just a big wish. If you look back to when you were young, you probably had more dreams, your dreams perhaps are not the same now, for example, a dream to be a doctor, a dream to be rich, a dream to have a hundred £100 million pounds when you are thirty 30 years old. The question is: Is your dream big enough? You will probably say "No, I cannot dream big" because it is not going to happen.

The truth is dreams are never too big for people to accomplish, nothing seems too outrageous. The world is yours. Reality is what others, someone else, for example, your parents or your lovers, want to keep you contained within. The most popular words you hear are: "You cannot do that", "Nobody has ever done that before", "It will never work". Unfortunately, you are a dreamer but could eventually become accomplished, having heard these things. You overcome them. You then refuse to accept some else's 'reality' for your own life.

Society (most people) let the average person live the average life, bound by fear, while they pursue your chosen future, your dream. The author would like to suggest not believing the people who tell you that you cannot or won't, because it is your dream, you really must believe it because your dream can be your future. There is some suggestion from Chris Widener (2002) that this is tremendously helpful for reminding and motivating you towards your dreams:

D is for Dare, dare to dream while others do not
R is for Relentless, pursue your dream no matter what
E is for Excellent, strive for excellence in all you do
A is for Abandon, abandon any other alternative plans
M is for Measure, constantly measure where you are in your dream journey.

These are great motivators for you, however, there are some practical tips in the next chapter which will be able to help you to make your dream come true and you will not have to live a mundane life.

Brian (2001) comments that: "You must dream big, because only big dreams have the power and energy to change your life". You must let yourself dream and imagine whatever you dream of, dream of the life that you want, dream of having what you want to have. The truth is you must dream if you want to make your dream come true.

There is a brilliant technique to help you to go through with your dream. Just imagine in the next five years, your life is absolutely perfect, how would that be? What would you be doing? Where would you be working? How much money would you be earning? How much money will you have in your savings account? And more importantly, how would you live your life?

You should imagine your life in the long term. Imagine how you would like your life to be. The magic is, the more you keep dreaming about your health, education, money, success and happiness, for example, the closer you will become to your success. The positive dream is the dream which is motivating you to be patient, to work harder, and encourages creativity in your brain in order for you to intelligently brainstorm. At the end, you will find your dream has happened and has become real for life.

It may be that now you know what your dream is, but the most important thing is how you are going to implement it into your life, describing if possible what your life purpose is. In order to describe your own life, you should be able to answer the following questions: 1) What is your dream for life? You might consider this in the area of 2) Why you are alive, 3) What is your life for? In order to find out what your purpose is in life, you are now required to look at your life goal. Again, it is not easy to clarify this goal.

Although, it is so difficult to make the decision of which dream you would really like to do, or which dream you have made up your mind to make come true and really happen, perhaps you have been waiting for it. As you may know, there are no courses or any universities in this world who would be able to teach you how to set up your own life's dream as life goals. According to Anthony Robbins, defining the dream is a powerful process for thinking about your ideal future, and for motivating yourself to turn the vision of the future into reality. The process of deciding what your dream is, helps you to choose where you want to go in life.

By knowing precisely what you want to achieve, you know where you have to concentrate your efforts. You will also quickly spot the distractions that would otherwise lure you from your course. More importantly, focusing properly on your chosen dream can be incredibly motivating, and as you get into the habit of deciding and achieving dreams, you will find your self-confidence grows fast. Dreams are set on a number of different levels. Firstly, create your 'big picture' of what you want to do with your life, and decide on a large scale what you want to achieve. Secondly, you may find smaller dreams within your big dream and you can make these your goals.

There is a special technique to help you; imagine your dream and place it as a goal in your life, then make it a target that you must hit, so that you reach your life time goals. Finally, once you have your plan, you can then start working to achieve it. So now, you should start the process of working towards your life time goals, and find out what it is that you can do today to start moving towards them. There are also some notes and tips for you to have a look at, revolving around what your current dream is. Is it big enough? Let's see.

The General Dream

Agriculture World's dream

In the early 18th century, the world entered into agriculture and a generation shared the workplace and the way of life. A result of this unique experience of these core, generational differences was that people dreamed of how they could own a piece of land for farming, including a hut or Bangalore for their living accommodation where it was safe enough to live.

The best job in those days was as a farmer, sharing the day to day life with everyone in the family. The size of family was very large, mother; father, brothers, sisters, sometimes uncles and aunts, grandmother and grandfather all lived together. Everyone in the family supported each other. Helping each other was such a great thing that people did, not helping out others was considered to be bad and unheard of. The world was slow going at the time.

The technology had not been developed as it is today. People now communicate with each other in an easy way, without the need of word of mouth. Simple letters and telegraphs seemed to be the best communication methods, used in villages, sub districts, districts, provinces and countries to communicate with others in the surrounding areas.

While it was realistic to dream, only a small number of people had dreams among members of any given generation. It was true that individuals from particular family generations shared and supported a common way of life that influenced values and attitudes. These made people dream small 'inside the box,' as this was the only experience people could have at that time.

The main reason to have those dreams was so that you were not different from others in society. This was ridiculous and lead to having a miserable life. Owning a piece of land to be able to farm which people could live on, was good enough in those days. Whoever owned a piece of land, as well as a hut or Bangalore, was seen as a very great success in life for those people in that generation.

Industry World's dream

The generation had changed in the late 18th or early 19th century. In those days, the way of living relied upon industry and factory work, for example, the steel factories. By the time the computer was introduced, in general, people dreamt of having a simple way of life by having their own house. It was so difficult for people in those days to have their own home. Many countries' governments supported people in having their own homes by providing them with benefits.

Having your own house was seen as such a big success. Owning your own vehicle and operating your own business was a really successful life. Ask yourself what kind of dream you have now. The most popular answer to this question, most people would confidently say, is to become very highly successful.

The truth was the world was cruel; the rich became richer in each generation. Everybody took advantage of others. The more you could take the more you achieved success. The way of general life in those days was that people only had to work and concentrate on themselves. The one man show was a great idea, the best was such a hero, and whoever could be the 'hero' was one of the best and most powerful in the life time of that generation.

High Technology World's dream

The high technology generation which happened in the late 1900s, was unlucky for those born in between the two generations from the 20th and 21st centuries, where the world has gone backwards in terms of people's relationships. People have to rely on each other; the one man show is not working any more. The world has now become smaller where poor become rich and the rich become poor all depending on how intelligent you are.

We are living in an intelligent world. Have you ever thought about this? What is your dream today? If your answer is to own a nice house, with an expensive car and to run own your business then the truth is, unfortunately, you are not living in the current world any longer. You are living in the old world which is the same as the last generation, the industrial world.

Please note that the new generation should be dreaming to have more freedom, freedom to show how intelligent you are, having dreams seem such an important part of this, where you can tell what kind of future you could have. The best dream for people in the 21st century should be something about a brand new idea. You should be able to show what a new innovator you are, how brilliant your ideas are, how different you are, how it is possible for you to help people, how friendly you are, and how good you are in terms of helping people to network, which is one of the most important parts of being alive in this world.

The more you connect to the network system, the more your chances of succeeding in whatever you should be doing. Achieving such a dream is seen as being very highly successful. The author suggests that this is one of the great tips that you should take into account, adapting these ideas into your own dreams and setting real goals for your life.

The first step in finding your goals is to consider your dream, what do you want to be? What could you achieve in the future? (The future should be a time of at least ten years or your whole life future). The most appropriate, incredible technique to make your dreams work, is to draw them on a piece of paper, so now you are required to write those dreams down. Here is an empty piece of paper with empty bubbles for you to write your dream down. You are now required to write as much as you like, do not worry too much if you cannot fill them all in.

Now supposing you have filled all of your circles with your dreams, it could be said that your imagination has now has transformed those ideas from your head (which are generally known as dreams) and put them into writing. You have gone through the process yourself and placed them on the paper where people (eye witnesses) can see, presenting your dream to let someone else know what you have been dreaming of for some period of time. In short, telling people what you dream of is one of the best commitments you can make for your own future.

The truth is no one can achieve anything if they try to achieve too many dreams at the same time. Having too many dreams can be distracting, affecting your concentration and focus, there would be too many goals to aim for, for whatever you are going to do. For this reason the author strongly recommends that you choose which dream has the most impact on your feelings.

Try this technique to cut them down: Close your eyes, one by one think of each dream, imagine that if you achieved each dream. Which one made you feel the happiest in the world in that moment? Which one made you feel the most excited about the life you are going to have? Score them from one to ten with the following details below:

Score Details
1. Just a dream, whether it can be achieved really does not matter in my life.
2. Because I have seen someone else have it or become what they want, then I would like to have or become it as well.

3. Good to become or have it, but unsure as to whether I am going to be very happy.
4. Might be good if I can become or have it.
5. Quite like it, but I don't think it's going to make any difference to my life.
6. Like it very much, but not really the best.
7. Liked it very much in the past, but I am not so sure now.
8. I like it and am happy to see myself becoming or having it.
9. Love it very much, I am going to be very happy if I have or become it.
10. Love it very much. I need it, without this, I would never be happy or would not feel 'alive' in my life.

Once you have scored them all, you should then delete the worst ones from the list, crossing them out by number.

Finally, this leaves you with the ones where you dreamed you were the happiest. The highest scored is the one you are going to keep. The author is now very happy to say that the world is going to be pleased and welcomes you to be one of the most recognised and successful in the world, of whatever you dream of. Therefore, you are now required to take a look at your dream that you have written down, and let the world know of what you have committed yourself to become in the very near and far future. Now is the time to implement your dream, setting it up as a life goal; somehow, this might not be easy to clarify.

There are no schools, colleges or universities to teach you about the goal of your future life. According to Anthony Robby, "The goal is a powerful process for thinking about the ideal future, and for motivating yourself to turn the vision of the future into reality."

The author now concludes that the dream should be something very positive. The process of setting goals will be able to help you choose what you want to achieve, you know where you have to concentrate your efforts. Finally, you should also quickly spot the distractions that would otherwise lure you from your course. More importantly, motivate yourself. As you get into the habit of setting and achieving your dream and your goals, you will find that your self-confidence will grow.

Chapter 3:

Discovering Your Talent

Talent

Talent is something that you naturally have, something that you have had since you were born. Brian Tracey (2003) states that: "The average person uses only 1% or 2 % of their brain for living and work. The rest is never used." This is something you do not need to achieve over night to make an impression on your life, just use your brain slightly more than you would normally use it.

The surprise is that you will be achieving success in using your own brain, which would make changing your whole life possible. Compare your brain to a knife. If you never use it, then of course it would never get sharp. If you start using it, you must then practice or sharpen it with stone everyday, then one day this knife will be so sharp that you can cut whatever you like. This can be applied to everything in your life.

In fact, it is the same as the way people live their lives. If you use your brain to think, to practice talking about your life, making plans, talking about your success, talking about your future life, then you could find out the best way to be able to achieve your goals faster. The author strongly recommends living this way, which would help you to achieve success faster than you thought you could. Napoleon Hill (2003) states, "The important key of the world's successful people is to find out first what you really love, and then to find out how you can really make it work."

This is one example of what the richest people in the world say, "I never work a day in my life." The truth is that they always look to find out what it is in the world that makes them really happy, and then they do it, and do it more and more. Elaura (2006) also says that: "The true successful people do not spend their lives trying to be what they are not."

Successful people always make good use of their talents. The reality is that most employers are always looking to employ someone who has attractive qualities, something that makes those people different. It could possibly be defined as talent, and is synonymous with anyone who is a "yes" person; most managers are satisfied with this. It is something that these employees contribute which is vital to having the ability to produce a product or deliver a service. 'Excellent talent' then refers to those who produce an above average amount of the product and 'poor talent' means those who do much less than average. For example, in sport, most managers always speak of quality of talent and identify those players who are essential to that success.

However, talent is something that can be identified by asking someone who has known you for a period of time. In fact, there are four techniques that could help you to find and improve your talent and demonstrate what talent looks like:

1. To identify what characterises a high performance. This is a quality of output, or the amount of number of defects created. It is the amount of revenue a sales group have generated. For example, when the work is hard and there are a lot of benchmarks to go by, people know more or less, who contributes the most to organisations.
2. Find the niche in which you perform best. Find someone who has spent some time with you. Try to find out from them what one thing encourages you to perform your best and in what. These could be competencies, activities which you engage in, attitudes or philosophies, education, or work methods or processes. Ask that person to look objectively to see if you have any of the distinguishing characteristics or anything in common with your high performance. It is right that having a certain college or university degree or grade point average, or even having a certain defined amount of experience is going to be a real discriminator of high performance. However, it is more likely to be something much more subtle and often a combination of factors that makes the real difference. It is finding these that will give you an edge in finding your best talents.
3. Find out where these high performances are located. To do this well requires a focus on your competitive intelligence. You can gather information and inspect and observe in you where they may be located. You can certainly use your friends, family and work friends and ask them to notice where these results come from. From everything you actually do, to your good performances and skill set, find out where most people see them in you. One of the most useful ways to find talent is to ask these questions which you should list and refer to.
4. Find out what will encourage these potential high performances from your work colleagues or school friends. Through discussion and observation, notice the high performance you currently have, and it should be possible for you to put on good performances. By focusing on what attracts high performance, you will also discover what you are not good at. For example, one friend might say that you are the best public speaker, but you are the worst at numerical skills. In fact, the most famous people are surrounded by others who love to see them perform their talent, so the talent shows easily. So observe your life activities and notice where your talents are shown in your normal activities. There are some more techniques which would help you to find out what you really talent is, this would help you to do whatever you like, encourage you to do it, again and again, and you would never tire of it. There are 8 questions you must ask yourself:
    1. What will make you the happiest? Where would you do it? Imagine if you had unlimited money, you have got enough money to spend, money is not a problem anymore. Whatever it is that you want to do, without being paid, you would still love to do it and you would never tire of it.

    2. What is the one thing that you have always been good at since you were young? (For example, singing, being good at persuading people, being friendly.)

What are the talents that you use in your daily activities that you most   often do to enjoy yourself or that have made you happy since you were born? Look at the talents that always get good comments from someone around you, who have known you for a long period of time.

3. Is it something very easy for you to learn, and easy to do?

4. Is it interesting to you, do you love it and love to think about it? Do you love to read about it or talk about it? Then you should find out what it is and apply it to your daily life and activities.

5. What is it you love about it from your deep in your heart? What would you absolutely love and would want to be the best in?

6. Whatever it is that you want, you should want it so much that everything else is secondary. You should enjoy it so much that you never want to stop to eat, or even sleep because you love to do it.

7. Lastly, think of someone that you love, like or respect. Think of someone who you would like to be most like. In fact, by imitating their traits or confidence, you could be as successful as him or her. Try to copy them as much as you can, and surely, one day you will be like him or her.

The key to successfully bringing out your best talent is, first of all to understand what it is and secondly, to create a list of high quality performances. Measure it so that you can determine your success rate. By asking people to score you, your observers (friends, family) will help you to find your talent source, what you are the best at and what is right for you. You will have developed powerful talent intelligence (Kathie and Steve, 2009).

Talent is a human resource which is special in that you should apply it to your life, rather than just using it without taking care of it, in aspects of daily life activities. Rather, talent can be applied to your life goals using the strategy of development, retention, concentration, motivation and focus. Sometimes, implementing your talent into your general activities can be a good use of your skills. At other times, it may be a waste of human resources.

Your first responsibility is to find your talents; it should attract and retain your interest. Without this primary function, you cannot achieve your full potential. Finding talents can be a difficult task, especially at times when not many people know you.

However, talent is something you have had since you were born. In fact, it was born with you, in your heart and in your life. However, there are other skills you may need, this means you should have those skills which you may or may not like but you must have them. This is because those skills are going to help you to get to the top of where you want to be. This is the best way to help you to achieve something. On the other hand, being the best at training is not important, but training to be the best is the perfect way to help you to succeed.

There are some brilliant techniques that you should practice: 1) Read about the things you like to do everyday. 2) Listen to those things in your car, or when travelling, think how many hours of your time you have spent travelling in a year. According to Brian Tracey (2005) in his book (Goal), most people spend between 500 to 1,000 hours a year travelling. You must change the way you spend your time when travelling and use the time to learn how to become the best in your occupation. 3) Lastly, you should join classes or take a seminar in the topic you are interested in to help you to climb to the top in whichever occupation you are in.

These are however, flexible techniques. This is one of the most important rules that you must be clear about - focus on your dream or goal, but do not fixate on the process of how are you going to succeed. Do not think about failing, there is nothing more dangerous as much as you being fearful of success. The fear of failure is one of the hardest barriers to overcome. In fact, the fear of failure should be looked at as a medicine to motivate you to get stronger. Being scared or frightened will stop you finding the way or the solution to success in your life.

The fact is that success is waiting for you; it is the opposite end of being unsuccessful. Please remember that failure is not your choice. Brian (2001) states that: "There are only 3% of world's population and in any country who can be successful; the other 97% never succeed in life." And the fact is that most of the people in the 97% always have an excuse for themselves. For example, "No I am nothing special or have no talents", "I am not good at this", "I am no good at that." In contrast, if you answer this question immediately then this probably means that you have already have an idea of who you are, and what people think about you.

According to Anthony Robbins (2009) says that: "Everyone must have something special of their own. However, now is the time for you to find out what your talent is. In fact, there is quite an easy way to find out what talent you have got. There is an appropriate way to find out what people's talents are, ask someone who has known you since you were born, or over a certain period of time. For example, two years or six months, whoever knows you well, such as school friends, family members, roommates or colleagues."

Now go and ask them or think very carefully of any of your work tasks or any activities you have done in the past, where most of the people around you have said that you are very good at doing these tasks. This is something that might not be concerned with what you are currently doing or working in at the moment. The truth is it does not matter whatever you are currently doing because at the time, you did not know what you wanted.

So now you need someone to score you in your previous activities, for example, working skills, languages or driving. Whichever activities or work you have done before over a period of time, you now need to list your activities where you always or often heard praise from those people. For example, 'excellent', then list about 10 names of your friends, family or colleagues. For each person or name, number them between 1 and 10, including your life activities. Shown in the table below:

Finding Talent Table

No	Activities	1	2	3	4	5	6	7	8	9	10	Total
	Singing	+	0	-	+	+	+	+	+	+	+	8+/1(0)/1-
1												
2												
3												
4												
5												
6												
7												
8												
9												
10												
	Total											

Meaning   + = Excellent   0 = Average   - = Poor

When you have completed the table above, have a look at where your talents are, look at the total score and which activity you have scored mostly '+'. This is most likely to be your talent. Congratulations! You now know what your talent is. So now is the time to transform your talent into your goals and plans. In order to make it work you will then put them in your plan for life.

After you have found your talent, the next thing to do is to manage your talent. You must integrate them in a way that is most advantageous to you. This may involve creating life goals or creating plans that are shared among other qualities you have got. This plan sharing takes the concentrated focus from your personality and requires something more practical than just having the qualifications. Furthermore, integration also means finding educational opportunities, whether as part of your normal working environment or through continuing other activities in your life.

Talent therefore, is not only about finding out what they are, but also educating and developing it in such a way as to be most beneficial to you. While people may work towards an opportunity through formalised education or work experiences, this falls short of true talent implementation, which involves a concerted effort of education through regular, practised activities meant to achieve certain levels. The benefits of having talent are often achieved more quickly, which may include people of young ages who go on to have a highly successful life. The author is hoping that this talent discovering should help you to identify who you really are, in the other words this should give you the answers as to where and what you should be doing in the future. This is something which is very valuable for your whole life. It is life's weapon which helps you to protect yourself from the dark, and to carry on living in this life full of energy and motivation.

Chapter 4:

Structuring and Organising Life

Seavey (2009) explains that the life structure of human life is the sum total of the ways in which it divides its dream or goals into tasks, and then achieves coordination between them. The human life is about dreams, goals, strategies, plans about experience, it link to their satisfaction and its relationship to the set of achievements between tasks, responsibilities and individual motivations. It might be difficult in reality to structure human life because it is highly complex.

Tell yourself this is the most wonderful moment or time to be alive. Tell yourself about the new you, new life, clear dreams and goals, new life with strategies and new plans. This is an opportunity; this is good news for your life. Indeed, this plan is a sign to demand the highest level in your field, whatever it is you do. You have the superior ability to influence yourself, to direct yourself in work, to serve yourself in leadership or in a team player capacity. You are the one who will fill these leadership positions in whatever organisation you are in. One of the best is you.

Have you ever thought about the following factors as you go about the core planning and scheduling of your own life? Most people generally operate physiologically at work; their energy levels can be low or high at different times of the day, the hunger factor, and what affect we all have on how people communicate. The space and environment affect people's creativity and responses. What is the best way? You need to know and prepare yourself to schedules your plans based on the present life.

Let's examine some basic truths about people that affect daily life, and see how to include these when you plan and schedule your own life. You need to think through what you mean to accomplish before you even schedule your life, and to organise your preparation, you need to take a look at the following pictures below.

Bamboo

Teak

Cut Bamboo

Cut Teak

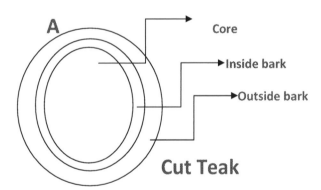

A

→ Core

→ Inside bark

→ Outside bark

Cut Teak

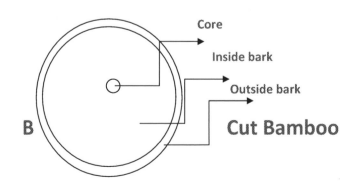

Core

Inside bark

Outside bark

B

Cut Bamboo

Bamboo is a plant, commonly grown in Asia. It is a type of grass with a 'hard', woody, hollow stem. Many different climates can support or destroy it, although it is commonly associated with the tropics. It can be used for construction material; it is a fast growing grass and can grow in dense conditions. It is considered to be one of the best renewable resources on the planet.

When it is cut, you may see the picture A & B that following by:

- The first section is the inside core. It is the core or main responsibility for the tree's life. This part is crucial, without it, the tree cannot survive. It is the main pipe which the tree needs, to send the food through to the rest of the plant. After the outside part has eaten the food, water and air, it generates energy and uses it for the whole of the tree, in fact, without this part the tree cannot stay alive.
- The second section is the inside bark. It is a necessary part of the tree, because this part helps to protect the tree. However, without it some trees can stay alive, some may not, it depends on how strong they are and the circumstances or environment that they are living in, it is better for the tree if it does have this bark.
- The third section is the outside bark. It acts as a skin to cover the inside and makes the trunk look attractive. It is not really the main or core element for the tree's life. Without this bark, the tree can still remain alive.

To analyse and compare a cut Bamboo and a cut Teak tree, if you look at the inside core of a cut Bamboo, there is an empty hole with nothing inside, the second bark is very thin and lastly, the outside bark is quite thin and hard and is a green colour. If you look at a cut Teak tree, the inside core is a large hard core of wood, the second bark is quite thin(but still hard) and certainly in the last section the outside bark is thin with hard wood.

Compare the two pictures to your life. This is a new idea and subject which most people ignore; in fact, it is a very complex side issue. Comparing these pictures of trees to your life is firstly about having the core to be alive, without this part you cannot live. What is it, the core of your life? Is it about your dream or goal of what you want to be or achieve? Living without this core means you are not alive.

You are living just to eat and breathe, but you are doing nothing to achieve any goals or a plan in your life. However, you must now think and compare the differences between these two trees, Bamboo and Teak. Imagine cutting these two trees, then comparing the differences. If you are looking at a cut Bamboo, there is nothing inside the first or core part.

There is a big hole inside. Knowing how Bamboo live, any storms, winds, floods in their environment will immediately have an impact on them. They may bend over to the left, or they might bend to the right. On the other hand, they live where it is very risky so they could easily die, because they are technically controlled by the external environment. The second part is quite thin, and the final part is quite thick and strong. They look good, have nice skin, and attract others to look at them, but actually, there is nothing inside at all. Comparing this Bamboo cut with your own life is quite dangerous because if you have no core or knowledge of what your life is for, then how do you know what you want to be? It means that the core of your life is too narrow or very small, which is dangerous because if any changes happen externally, for example, politically with government rules and regulations, these could have an impact on you and force you to settle or live a stable life.

Now is the time to look at the cut Teak. Surely, you know how big a core they have (inside the first part)? Teak is the best and strongest wood in the world. Comparing your life, go to the first part, the first inside part, namely the core. It is very large and would take a hundred years to grow and live, followed by the second part, the bark, which slim and thin.

Teak tends to have a long life such as a hundred years. It grows well and strong and is rarely impacted by anything, such as storms, flooding or wind. They are strong enough to stand up, telling the world I am what I am. They stay focused on building their body, the muscles and brain. The core and body are the most valued wood in the world, for human accommodation, houses and buildings.

There is no such thing that could easily destroy them. Imagine you are these two types of trees living in the present life or in a situation at work. Given the picture and the issues, here you might able to compare the following points to your own life.

'Finding the Core for Life' Table

Part	Description	Yours
Core, first section inside You must fill in yours to see what you need to know. It is your responsibility, to help you to be the best in any occupied situation that you are engaged in. Please note: In reality, this part is very important. Many people may not realise that what they really need to know, which is that they should be at the top of whatever they do or become.	You need to know this. You need it for your strategy, or to be able to use it to achieve you goal or be successful in life. Without this knowledge you may not live or survive in whatever you do. For example, if you are a hotel receptionist, you must know how to assign rooms to your guests, without this you might not be able to do your job or grow in your career.	
Inside bark, the second section This part is also important. It helps you to know yourself better. However, it does not mean that without this part you cannot live. Therefore, this part is sometimes to convince you to look after yourself better and support who you really should be.	You should know yourself better; if not then your life may not really be happy or any better. For example, in education or an occupation, knowing which football team won the FA Cup this year, is not going to have any impact on your job, unless you work or are concerned with the sports industry	

Outside bark, third section Please note in reality it is quite dangerous because most people like to spend so much time watching football games, drinking, or talking about life, this is something you do not need to do or know. Whether or not you know about them, is not going to improve your quality of life. Perhaps without knowing, this part your life might be better than what you think it currently is.	Whether you know or not, does not really matter, knowing who won Big Brother, does not really matter if your job or work life is nothing to do with it.	

If your goal is to be the guest service department manager in a hotel, where you currently work as a receptionist, then if you respond to your dominant set of motivations by knowing what qualifications you should have, for example: languages, a good personality, good communication skills and management skills. Therefore, this is a core for your present life where you have learned, practised or already know how to work or deal with the job, because you have experienced it.

To know the cleaning process for the room attendants is not that important, but if you do know then it is something of an advantage to you, if not, it really does not have a negative impact on being a guest service manager. If you do know these things, then it's an advantage for you which would possibly put you in a better position than the other guest service managers from the other hotels. (Inside bark/second section) Finally, knowing how Tesco operate their store does not really matter to you (outside bark).

People are encouraged externally to know pointless information; this is just a waste of their lives. In fact, this is the dangerous part; people spend too much time talking or knowing something which really does not matter to them. Be aware, this is just gossip; too much time spent watching TV, is something that does not really matter to him or her, but is something that people love to do, but ultimately will be a waste of your life.

Surprisingly, this could result in you becoming lazy and not bothering to do the things that you are supposed to do, for the better or to improve your life. So knowing your own core of what you are and what you really want to be, learning what to do to help you to improve the process, helps you to succeed or to be the top of your occupation. This is one of the important tasks that you need to look at, so that you know what will help you to succeed faster and have better success in life.

There is one very good example, Michael Jackson. He wasn't born into a wealthy family, yet he had a really big dream since he was five years old. Continuing to do what he needed to be doing, implementing his talent, continuing to improve the skills he needed (dancing and singing), he never spent much of his spare time talking about someone else's life. He just concentrated on what he was doing. As a result, he had become the world's King of Pop and a super star when he was just 30 years old and remained so up until the end of his life.

He had an incredibly amazing career in what he was doing, most people in the world looked at him as the world's greatest and most successful singer. People never realised how tough it was being Michael Jackson until the end of his life, when he passed away on the 25th June 2009 at just 50 years of age.

Think carefully about why he had such a successful and amazing career. One simple answer to this question is: he had been himself, using his talent, he had been what he had wanted to be, he had known what he wanted to be since he was five years old (young kid). It took him 30 years to become successful and stay at the top as the world's King of Pop.

Think carefully, this is the same thing. Compare you own life with Michael Jackson's life, why can't you be the best in what are you doing now? Think carefully about how many years have you spent on your career. Are you doing something that is really who you are? Are you doing it because you love to do it? If you did not get paid today, are you going to carry on working or doing what you are doing now? If you have these answers then congratulations, you seem to know what you want and success is waiting for you in the near future.

This life planning can help you figure out what you want out of life and how to get there. It will help you to make plans for your own life, which supports your own choices. There are some primary goals which every life needs.

If you have a life goal like this, use this book to see what you have (talent), what you need (strategies and tools), and what action (plans) or steps to take to reach your goal. This book can help you to accept that you are what you are, a whole person, with many ideas and goals. This is true no matter who you are, what you are, what hard times you have had or are still having, as long as you have plans. Now you can go forward in a better way and get on with your own life.

This book is for people who are looking to improve the quality of their lives, looking for the way and how to succeed in life, and finally who are looking to discover a new world for themselves. A life plan is basically an idea or a plan of what you would like to do, what kind of life style you would like to have, what quality of life you would like to have. More importantly, it is about the dream you want to make happen or come true.

It helps you look at every important area that you probably never realised before. This will help you to set new goals, or make some changes, and most importantly, will help you to discover strategies of how to get there.

It may seem too hard to think about all of these things when you first read this book. It might help you to remember that nobody makes these changes all at once. You must pick one goal to work on at a time, the one that makes you the happiest and where success for you is possible.

Time for Life to Change

Many people have been there, most people make promises to themselves that this year will be different. Most people will lose weight, people will exercise, people will make friends, and people will get jobs and make it into university. Most of us mean to follow through, but something bursts our bubble and we do not make the change.

There are many reasons why people give up on goals, some of them are; not really being ready for change, trying to do something too fast, not taking care of yourself along the way. Then we fail, we feel worse about ourselves and the vicious cycle begins. If these sound familiar, here are a few things you have to keep in mind. Life is too short; the average life span is 65 for women, and 75 for men. So let's calculate for 70 years average, meaning you will be alive until the age of 70. That is 365 days multiplied by 70, which is equal to 25,550 days.

Therefore, making a life change takes small and big steps the further you go in time. You must only make a plan that will motivate you along the way. No matter how hard you try or how good your plans are, obstacles are to be expected. Do not give up, concentrate and focus, if you fail first time this does not mean that you won't ever be able to reach your goal.

The best technique for sticking with your life plan is remembering that it won't always be this hard. Part of the process should include time for relaxing, having fun, and staying connected with people who give you hope. Life change may not be quick, but it can be rewarding overtime.

Planning Your Goal

Now you're ready to make the goals or steps and the strategies you need to take to reach your goal. For example, if your goal is to get a good job, some of your plans might be;

- Find an employment consultant
- Do a job assessment
- Pick the type of job you want
- Get job support
- Learn how to write a cover letter and resume

If your goal is to make a friend, some of your plans might be;

- Make a meal for people you live with
- Smile or talk to a stranger every day

If your goal is to make yourself rich, some of your plans might be;

- Find what business you would really love to do
- How are you going to achieve your business?
- How are you going to start your business?

However, you also have to prepare the list of obstacles to your goal. You will need help with these things to succeed in your goal. For example, if your goal is to move into a new apartment, some of your obstacles might be;

- You cannot afford the security deposit
- The place you would like to live is far away from your hometown
- The monthly rent might be expensive, you cannot afford it

Now you may have to list the resources you need to support your goal. These things might be internal or external to you, which will keep you motivated along the way. For example, if your goal is to go university, some of your internal and external resources might be;

- You like to learn new things
- Your school can help you identify the best university for you
- You stick with what subject you are going to study

Setting Target Years and Dates

For each of your tasks, set a year and date and a certain stage by when you will finish it. Evaluate how successful you will be at each stage; try to give yourself plenty of time to avoid putting undue pressure on yourself. Start by reviewing the step or target, resources and obstacles you prepared for planning for your life change.

Petersen (2003) suggests trying to set dates and years that allow you plenty of time to do what you need to do, depending on your life goal. Some steps or tasks may takes years, even ten years to complete. Remember that the dates and years are not set in stone. The point of the dates and years is to keep you focused on moving forward. Sometimes you will find that the task takes more or less time than you thought it would.

This is common; it simply means that you should adjust your dates to fit how long a task is really taking, once you start doing it. It is also one of the reasons, the author recommended in the beginning of this book, that you review your plans every 6 months. Regular reviews will allow you to adjust plans to fit what's going on in your life.

Congratulations! It is now time to start completing the steps to reach your goal. It is also important to make sure that you are still taking care of yourself each day. Sometimes, your plans start to fall apart when you are taking care of yourself physically, emotionally and spiritually. If you feel discouraged, look again at your dream in chapter two of this book, where you chose a set goal or plan for yourself; if you have stopped following your plans, you may want to put aside your life goal tasks and focus on something else.

You may close your eyes. Jessica and Judith (2004) comment that using imagination techniques where you can see yourself succeed in whatever you want your future to be. Without following your plan, perhaps your dream might become a sleeping dream as many people's do. Stop it and get back to your plan, motivate yourself, you are going to be what you are going to be. Please note do not be afraid to ask for help.

Life Success Diagram

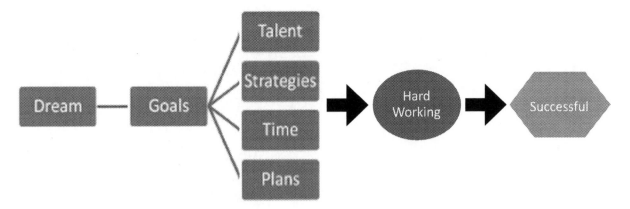

Accordingly, with a review of the literature and the findings of this diagram, it appears that you should have transformed your real dream - only the one that you have made in your mind today. However, it is noted that by just supporting the dream will not make it come true, you must place it as a goal, you may implement your talent, make strategies, follow proper plans, and go along with spending time on it.

According to Caetano (2002), he suggests that hard work is one of the important key elements in becoming successful, keep focusing on the goal going directly to its destination, where you can expect to be 100% satisfied with the achievement. Because human nature is always changeable and is often based on emotions, the successful expectation and satisfaction in your life is very difficult to measure. The author has used the successful parameter tool to measure your achievement and satisfaction which you can see in the next chapter.

Life Tree Innovation of Life Designs and Analysis

The purpose of this analysis is to see whether the life style you have used, its designed objectives and alternatives may be the choice or specific picture in your imagination. Any decision from the choice or life style should be explained, which strategy you were achieving in your performance and targets, which can be carried forward and entered to the account, to which well-formed part of the goals for the future operating period.

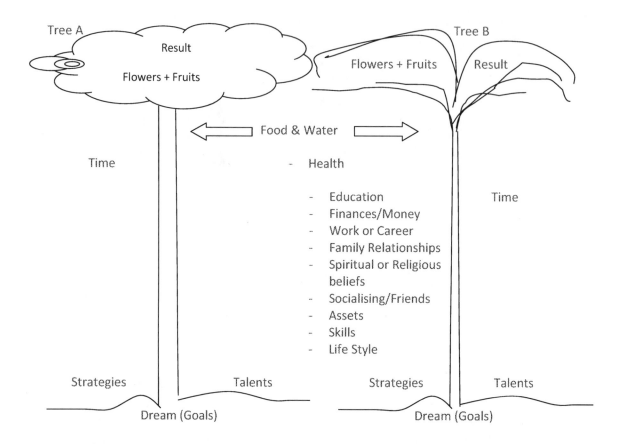

The life tree is an innovative creation confidentially based on the author's life experience. Some of the areas the author has worked in include; life development, change, strategy and developing vision and values, taking a holistic view in helping you with organisational development. Baldauf (1996) suggests that: "With approach balances theory and practice, grounded in experience." This can help you achieve your objectives by using the tree picture methods, cutting edge thinking and comparison tools.

This chapter encourages you to work with the facts and to take a look at your potential, responsibility for your relationships and accountability for your results. Working on your own, this will help you to focus on your goal, and learn to connect with and release your natural potential talent. While the life tree helps you deliver results, your input is designed to provide a foundation for sustainable growth and development, which continues long after you have your chosen your life style.

The author takes your life style as seriously as you perform. It is also in your interests to identify the best natural resulting life style for you, the author understands your concerns about outcome and reality. Vibrant dreams can be achieved through the knowledge and power of talent and strategy, and you are doing something about it, through your comprehensive line of premium-quality performance supplements.

Brown and Doolittle (1995) comment that the Life Tree is a life design and analysis tool to help you to analyse your life style, and benefits with an activity-driven view of how your dreams, goals, strategies and plans can help you to achieve. Without this model, you will be critically flawed and this could result in you having inappropriate objectives or targets.

To retain the profit and benefits of the goal, you should directly improve the bottom line dreams and goals. In fact, the dream is the root of your life. If your root is strong enough, (for example big and large) this means that you can hold your body upright and be strong enough to grow, to be able to fight and win when the storm or any disaster hits.

Dreams are the core of your performance. If you have a big dream then you would work hard to achieve it. It is the same in that if your roots are strong enough, they would help the tree to build on his or her body and grow. Big dreams are the root of being successful. Once your dream is well rooted, it will transform into a goal and be set up as your life target. The body of the tree whether big or small, would be the core of the dream, finding the talent and implementing it into strategies, preparing it as a weapon to fight for life.

You also need good food, clean water and clean air to help you to grow. It is the same in that you need good health, good education, good finances, good work, good skills, good family relationships and support, good spiritual beliefs, good assets and a good life style. The truth is all of these support you to grow stronger and have a higher level of success. The beliefs and motivations are a part of your life, like an energy or power to push and pull you to get closer to your success.

Time is also absolutely one of the major impacts which we cannot do anything about. The success is a result of your performance, which appears as fruit, flowers, leaves or wood. If you have a bigger success, then you can share your success with others. Give them an advantage to enhance their own successful lives. It is the same for the Teak. For example, it has a big body, tall with loads of leaves. The shadow of their leaves helps many lives, like the ant or the rat who use it to protect themselves from the rain.

Teak wood is one of the best and strongest woods in the world, helping millions of human lives, allowing humans to use their wood to build houses. The results you can see are the benefits of a big success, actually there are other benefits too. So you have nothing to prevent you or to stop you from moving forward to grasp your success in your hand.

The Life Tree B, in contrast, is the tree with the slim body, because the root or core of life is too small. This is the same when compared with human life. It is like someone who has no dreams. Of course, you would probably say "No, I have a dream". Surely, everyone would like to think that they have a dream, but think carefully. If you have a dream, but the dream you have is in your head, if it is never transformed onto paper, it will never materialise, it will never be set up as a goal for life.

In fact, this is a death dream, of which there is no point in having. It never works because you never think it is going to work. If a dream is just a sleeping dream, you might be happy when you dream, but unfortunately, it is not there when you are awake.

The body of your tree is so slim, because you haven't got a big or long enough root to help you to stand up, to push and pull you to have a bigger and taller life. You haven't tried to work hard, or you have never used your talents to help you to get good food, clean water, good health, a good education and clean air. This is something that you haven't tried.

Certainly, the outcome is quite simple. You have got a small flower, small fruits, and less leaves compared with the others. Finally, you cannot help anybody else or protect others' lives, because you are not bothering to think about it, or maybe you would but you are not strong enough to get what you want.

It is noted that you would probably feel very ashamed when you look back at your past. The reality is that time has gone too quick. Minutes, hours, days, months and years always go by, time never stops passing, even when you sleep. There is nothing you can do to stop time passing on this planet. Think carefully what kind of tree you would like to be, A or B.

The author hopes that you all are going to decide which tree to pick- type A, or B, it is entirely up to you. However, there is nothing wrong with choosing type A or B, remember; ultimately, the life you choose is yours.

Chapter 5:

How to Set Up Your Goal

David (1959) describes that a goal is an objective, a purpose, which is more than a dream. It is a dream acted upon. A goal is more than a haze; it is a clear goal that you are going to work towards. Schechner (1998) also comments that goals are part of basic human behaviour; they link to human skills which transform everyday life. Organising your individual life performance, using personal skills involved in the performance, bears responsibility for it helping the performance to become successful.

However, implementing your dream into goals can help you to grow faster. In fact, humans use goals in every stage of the thought process. From inventions, large and small, medical discoveries, engineering triumphs to business successes, all were first visualised before they became realistic. Satellites circle the earth not because of an accident, but because scientists set the conquering of space as a goal. Nothing can happen, no steps forward can be taken until a goal is established.

In reality, without individual goals you merely wander through your life. You stumble along without knowing where you are going and consequently you never get anywhere. David (1959) states that goals are as essential to success as air to life, no one ever stumbles into success without a goal, and no one ever lives without air.

Get a clear notion of where you want to go. For example, at the age of nine, the author always had dreams and goals; to graduate with a master's degree from a UK university. The reality was that the author was living with a poor family; there was no such education, not even secondary school. Sometimes the family had no money to buy food. But the author later graduated with a master's degree from the University of Birmingham, United Kingdom at the age of 27 years old.

This is what the author would like to say about goals, and always uses this slogan in life: "The most important way to look at people is; do not look at what they are or what they were, but always look at what they want to have or what they want to be." This should be more important than what he/she looks like.

People should learn a precious lesson by looking ahead both in life and in business. People should plan at least ten years ahead. You must form an image now of the person you want to be ten years from now, believe it, if you are to become that image.

The reality is to achieve any goal always takes time. Many people give up what they want to be or achieve because of this reason. Therefore, stay focused, be patient and motivated. This is very important; in order to support your success of any goal after it has been set.

Remember; know what your goal is today, you will achieve it perhaps in ten years time. No matter how other people see you now. No matter what you are or what you were in the past. Day to Day, make your mind up about what you want to be. This will be your direction, it will show you where to go, help you to see your destiny clearly in the future.

It is critical to think about to planning ahead, it is just another technique. An individual like you should be setting long term life goals; they will most certainly help you succeed faster in life. The truth is without a goal you cannot grow.

Next is the most important lesson for you to learn in life. The discussion of how to set your goals and the author believes this is the most important lesson - for you to plan your own career. Of course, before you start, know where you want to go.

This is a progressive business plan, but this plan is a life business, which, in a sense is a business unit. Your talents, skills and abilities are your weapon. You should actually develop your weapons, forward planning will help you improve your probability in becoming the most successful you can be. Here are the important techniques, which will help you to go forward at each stage for your whole life time. There are ten planning guides, which are the important parts of people's lives, without all these you may not know how to live successfully.

Using the imagination technique, which is one of the best and easiest methods to help you motivate yourself, persuade yourself to see a picture of how happy you will be, being a successful person in the world.

Please note, success requires effort, your heart and soul, and you can only put your heart and soul into something which you really desire. Switching from what you do not like to do, to what you do like to do is tantamount to putting a million horsepower motor in a ten year old car.

The dream of what you really want to be and desire to become can be carried forward from your dream section (previous chapter). But make sure it really is your desired dream.

However, the author has a special technique which gives you a weapon to use against committing your success suicide. The author suggests destroying them because they are dangerous for your life and future. There are five diseases you have to destroy very quickly before you can take further your life process and follow your dream as a goal to achieve in life. These are the following:

1) Self-depreciation - it is the negative self depreciation disease which always stops people having a successful life. It is a negative block to your success if you let this disease take you over. You have probably heard a hundred people say, "I want to be a doctor, artist, business owner, but I cannot do it", because "I am not intelligent", "I do not have support", "I am not rich", "I have no education", "I have no experience", "I don't know". These are the most dangerous and negative types of self

depreciation. They destroy your desire for your own life, stopping you from following what your heart really loves and wants.

2) Security- this is something people are happy with. Many people are happy where they are, with what they are, enjoying living life on a day-to-day basis. If you say "I have got security where I am", the unfortunate thing is, this is the most dangerous disease. The security disease will murder your dreams and your goals. It can stop you having a better life in the future; ultimately, it can murder your life. Do not let this disease come close to you. The reality of the world is that you can easily measure people by their activities: they very often get to work late, have no exciting daily life activities, they don't enjoy being at work and never look to find a way to improve their quality of life.

3) Competition - the thing is most people generally think that what they want to do, what they want to be or dream to be, that the dream or imagination has been created from their own previous self experience or someone else's experience. Bear in mind achieving anything in this world is down to the people who have created or made it. Rarely has it been naturally made. There are some people who let their dreams go, by saying; "The field is already overcrowded", "There are too many people doing this", "There is already someone doing want I want to do".

The reality is people are always fighting other people to get to the top. They are all fighting to be the best and to stay alive. Of course this is crucial, people are always fighting to survive and to stay alive. If you do not want to fight, if you do not like to fight or if you are afraid to fight, then you should not be alive today and you are not going to survive in this cruel world.

If you say: I cannot do that because someone else is doing it, then this disease will immediately kill you and stop you from being what you want to be or do. Think carefully, you are not alive if you do not fight.

4) Parental Dictation- being yourself is not that easy, especially when you are young and even when you are adult. We have all been told that the best people we should listen to, from the cradle to the grave, is our parents. Parents are always giving you the best advice and the benefit of their experience. In fact, advice is sometimes called 'order'. We get used to being told what to do when we are young, and still carry on listening to our parents when we are older, because that is what good people are supposed to do.

The parents have chosen the best for their children. They themselves have chosen because they have their own reasons or thought that was for the best. Of course, most parents want to see their children succeed, but the truth is the parents want them to succeed in a way that they see as success.

Think carefully who is going to be happy or proud of you, you can certainly now answer, yes the parents. The sad thing is - who is supposed to be living your life? Who is going to continue being alive in years to come? (In general, parents die before their children). Without the parents, how could children be alive in the first place? And without children can the parents live? The author has heard a hundred young people explain their career choice with "I would really love to do something else, but my parents want me to do this, so I must." Or some say "I have to become a doctor for my parents, because they wanted me to be a doctor when I was young". The truth is intelligent parents want to see their children live successfully.

If you are a young person or adult you should patiently explain why you would prefer a different career, and if you make your parents listen patiently, the author believes there will be an appropriate compromise, where balance and satisfaction should be met. The objectives for your future career, of both you and your parents, should be identical for you to gain success. But not being what you want to be is one of the most importance diseases to stop you from being a successful person.

5) Family Responsibility- the attitude of being with your family means a great deal to your life, but you should not let your family stop you from living your life. Your wife, your partner, your children, your lover, or whoever in your family, should be supporting you to be what you want to be, but you must not let them stop you from being what you want to be or to become a success in life.

There is no reason for anyone to be taking over or having power over your life. If you say "I would have been wise to change over five years ago, but now I have got a family and I cannot change." In fact, this illustrates that it is a kind of disease which will kill you for being alive.

This point increases your energy when you set a desired goal and resolve to work toward that goal. Goals cure boredom and chronic ailments. Goals are a physical power; they establish the energy and enthusiasm needed within you, something equally valuable is "automatic instrumentation" which is needed to keep you going straight towards your objective.

The most amazing thing about a deeply entrenched goal is that it keeps you on course to reach your target. This is double work, when you surrender to your goal; the goal works itself into your subconscious mind, which is always in balance. Your subconscious mind is then thinking, with its full cooperation. A person can be hesitant, confused and indecisive. Now with your goal absorbed into your subconscious mind, you will react right away, automatically. Your conscious mind is then free for clear, straight thinking.

The Real Goal For You

Like magic, the most important thing to help you to succeed in general is your real goal, clear thought and 100% desire. The real goal is directly related to a level of your success throughout your whole life. Whatever you want to be and do, it is always linked. The truth is ladies and gentlemen; whoever is successful always invests their time to find out what their real goal is.

Have you ever dreamt, for example, about having a big posh house? Excellent, because a dream is a goal as is destiny. You just do it, work on it, and then you will get it. The goal, in fact the real goal, is something that must be of the best quality and just for you, not for anyone else. But it does not mean that you are not going to do anything for anyone else. Whatever you want to be or do you must start from yourself then start walking forwards.

One of the most important questions for you to answer is what do you really want to be or do? What do you really want to do with your life? Remember, you cannot shoot anything if you cannot see what you are going to shoot. The best technique is for you to repeat (your goal as your destiny), asking yourself again and again every month and year - what do you really want to do? The best technique should give you the same answer; it is no good setting a goal if you keep changing your goal.

Goals or dreams can seem like unreal dreams, and far from the reality. Now it is your responsibility and your destiny to make your dreams come true. Put your dream on paper and more details will be further explained in the next chapter. You must place your dream in a box with your previously desired dream (which you made in the first chapter).

What dream have you made today?

This is the most important technique so try to be creative in writing your own life plan. This plan is a life action plan on how you can achieve your goals. This is going to be your life plan and 'to do list' and you need to take action according to this plan every day. The key to gaining success in life is to do what you should, in order to get closer towards your dreams and goals each and every day.

If action is not moving you toward your goals, the author would then like to suggest that you should change your strategies and start all over again. There is also another important technique that you must follow: you must be able to collect enough data concerning your project of which you must be knowledgeable about, in all aspects.

By choosing the best selection, you should be able to come up with several options and solutions and then select which will be the best to lead to your goals in life. You know nothing comes easily and each goal needs work.

Chapter 6

Health Planning

There are at least ten major areas that you should be considering to achieve. These are your life tools where your health comes first. This is an obvious thing to start with in everyone's lives, "The truth is no one is going to achieve or have success in anything without being healthy." The condition of your body and mind will help you to get the best out of you and you will be able to use them to your full potential. In fact, this will enable you to cooperate and change your life to help you to achieve major results. This practical advice can help you to achieve a fitter and healthier body.

Health is something you might have, but could be something you need to work for, and maintain for your entire life. It's an attitude, a state of mind, and a life-long goal. Health is one of those things that people tend to take for granted. Until you are facing disease or injury, your good health, like a clean house, goes unnoticed when all your body parts are working properly. There is no pain to grab your attention, no chronic illness to debilitate your daily life.

Actually, health is a state of mental and physical well-being. When everything is functioning properly, you experience a general feeling of vitality. Good health allows you to perform the tasks necessary and desirable to your daily life. Work, family, home and pastimes can be enjoyed and conducted without pain or interruption.

Good health is so important, about which you are surely not going to argue, because it allows you to focus on your interests and obligations. Imagine having poor health, in the form of injuries, disabilities, chronic pain, mental illness or disease. It prevents millions of people from supporting, caring and expressing themselves effectively. You might ask anyone who has lived with chronic pain and they will tell you how the condition clouds every aspect of your life, making even the most mundane tasks into ordeals with suffering and despair.

Also, mental illness and addictions are just as unhealthy as any other debilitating disease. Judgement and ability are lost, efforts wasted and relationships destroyed as the patient flounders through life, incapable of regaining that good health they thought was their birthright. For the majority of people who suffer with poor health, it is the loneliness and despair that ultimately destroys their lives.

On the other hand, people who are vibrantly healthy seem to attract success and respect without effort. Perhaps it is the same in life, people who constantly seek a superior mate or partner who fauns over them and offer special treatment to the athletically fit, do not do the same for unhealthy people. People who are healthy get promoted at work more readily, they are treated better socially and professionally and they tend to gain more respect.

Clearly, there are exceptions to every rule. Theodore Roosevelt was wheelchair bound and led the most powerful nation on Earth. These are, however, the exceptions. Good health is important because it makes your life more productive, social, strong and physically bearable.

In conclusion, good health gives you control over your own life. Being healthy is important for everyone's lives. Health is important for numerous reasons. For one simple truth is that you are not going to achieve whatever you want to be if you do not have a good health, whatever your dream is. It does not matter how big they are, there is no chance that you would get there. In contrast, if you are fighting to live because you are severely ill, then that is not the case.

Health is the ability to cope with everyday life activities and physical fitness, the fact is that if you do not have good health there is no quality of life. You must accept that normal health should be regarded as the most valuable asset that you must have and enjoy. In short, happiness results from certain actions - good fortune and health. Health is perhaps the most important gift that has been given to you next to the breath of life, and you shouldn't take it for granted that you will live a long, happy and prosperous life. Be aware, many people might say you are what you eat, and what you eat does affect your health.

John (1999) suggests that if you are going to succeed, you need energy. Energy is a prerequisite of motivation. Get enough sleep and you will get more done, in less time if your body is rested. Eat well regularly, have fun during your leisure time. Psychologists say that, to be highly motivated people need a healthy balance of work and play. Recognise that there is as much energy in emotional aspects of life as there is in the physical aspect.

In fact, you should develop a healthy self-image. Understand who you are and what you are capable of accomplishing and life becomes less threatening. You should avoid comparing yourself and your performance with your co-workers, friends or colleagues. The only meaningful comparison is between what you are now and what you can become.

You should also develop fulfilling leisure activities. If you do not have fun in life, you will be bored. Boredom is a dead battery, your body functions slow down and you will feel sluggish. John (1999, p. 88) says "Develop a loose schedule of activities for your day off, so you do not lapse into passivity. You should get involved in quality recreation, activities and physical fitness and do it just for the fun of it."

You should actually look inside yourself to something you are interested in (internal interest) and outside yourself for other interests (external interest.) Talk to someone about what you are interested in. Discover what you should be doing to make yourself healthier and have fun or enjoyment in your life. For example, join the gym, a social club or an exercise club.

This will empower you; do not wait for someone else to give you the power to improve yourself and to live your life in a more effective way. If you want to be creative and productive, you must be empowered. Empower yourself and become highly motivated, you need a healthy balance of work and play. "Recognise that there is as much energy in the emotional aspects of life as there are in physical aspects." (John, 1999)

However, now is the time for you to seek wealth, and the right time for you to find it. Please note: do not leave it too late to get back to being fit and healthy. In today's society, being grossly overweight or obese and living a wealthy life style has become the status quo. It has become almost acceptable, with most people being apathetic about it. But if you don't change your unhealthy life style, the consequences will cause you to pay dearly for it, in more ways than you ever imagined.

The US surgeon general reports that approximately 40% of US adults use tobacco regularly and almost half of the teenage group (13-19) smoke. The UCLA Rand Centre found that smoking leads to a 21% rise in health costs and a 28% rise in medication costs. More than 430,000 die each year from smoking. (Brian, 2001)

Find out more about your health at present. Measure yourself by how often you normally exercise a week, how often you normally go to see your doctor for your health check, and how happy you are with your health and life. Measure it yourself, then place it as one of the important primary goals for you to achieve.

Please note within different ages, health can be affected in different ways, so choose the sport you are most interested in. For example, with tennis, at the age of 21, you could take a beginners course twice a week. If you are 35, you could already be a good player, so play more often. At age 45, you might be more likely to play it as a hobby, twice a week. So, now is your time to think about what kind of sport you like most, pick one of them now and set it up as one of your life goals by filling in the table below.

Stage: year of age	Goal to achieve for Healthy	Process of How to do it?	Score (you must come back when you are at each of stage in certain age, then score yourself) Score from 0 – 10 which 10 is very successful, and 0 is completely fail
A: 16			
B: 21			

44

C: 25			
D: 35			
E: 45			
F: 55			
G: 65			
H: 75			

Chapter 7

Education Planning

Education is something of an essential component of life. It is a self-enlightening process that brings about an awareness of the world around you. It develops your perspective of gaining knowledge which opens up limitless opportunities, improving the academic aspects of life. While some say that education merely points out the process of gaining information about the world you live in, some say that the procurement of knowledge is mainly caused by having the right education, so why is education so important? The answer is quite simple- because it covers valuable life lessons and more.

In fact, since you live in an information age that is mostly marked by industrial labour and professional careers in various fields, especially in today's climate, employers are more likely to employ people who have finished college or university. Individuals who have accomplished post graduate studies are of great advantage. While individuals who have completed a degree are not likely to encounter difficulties in landing the job that they want, people who have never had a degree are expected to have one.

Today, the reality of education is a tool of defence when it comes to career survival and success. When it comes to education, school primarily dictates the subjects to learn. While it provides the fundamentals to specialise in certain fields of interest through specific degree courses, it takes time and commitment for it to be acquired. However, not all aspects of education are learned within the walls of schools. Education can also be acquired through experiences.

It basically paves the path towards getting a clearer picture of life, building confidence and courage to make decisions and face life's success and failures. In fact, for any individual, education is important to both your personal and professional life. Whether or not you are ambitious enough to dream of reaching a particularly high level of success, it has the capacity to become career leverage, which explains one of the main reasons as to why education is so important.

Completing advanced levels of education is an indicator of a great drive and commitment to learn and applying knowledge on a variety of tasks. Hence, the more you learn, the more knowledge you have, the more you earn. For instance, careers in the hotel industry, which is one of the strongest and fastest growing industries in the world, are hiring people who finished college degrees in hotel-related courses and enjoy salaries from £15,000 to £30,000 annually.

Education is equally important to people's financial growth. By having all the instructions on how to manage or handle money and invest it wisely, one can easily set up a business with minimum risk of going bankrupt. In this way, people who are tired of constantly pleasing the boss can turn to running their own business to enjoy greater flexibility and a stable income.

Lastly, one of the reasons why education is so important is its capacity to make hiring people easier and more convenient. Posting a particular requirement on the educational attainment of applications allows the employer to narrow down his search for qualified and able employees.

Many of today's employers value a college degree or college education above anything else. This applies even to positions that previously did not require a particular college degree or educational attainment. Hence, education has become both a barrier and advantage to landing great careers and ultimately succeeding in life. The author is really passionate about education. The author believes that education in relation to eradicating poverty can be broken down into four major categories:

1. Educating the young. They deserve strong, passionate, creative and productive teachers who can educate them well. If they don't know what is happening in the world around them, how can they do anything in the future? If you are reading this, chances are you already have a social conscience, and already care about eradicating poverty.
2. Schools for the poor, schooling can break the poverty cycle. If you get an education, you can get a better paid job and you can get out of the poverty cycle. If you get a great education, work hard and are smart, you can become teachers, doctors or politicians and influence the future of your country.
3. Agricultural development and sustainability. If villagers know how to properly farm and use their natural resources, they can increase the quality of their trade, and lessen the chance of natural disaster completely ruining their social structure.
4. Politics and education. It is great to trust the government, but you need to make sure your government know how to use the money and channel it back to your citizens in your country.

In conclusion, education is one of the important life tools which is obviously measured by qualifications and experiences. These come from formal education such as schools, colleges or universities (including direct learning) and from informal education, directly from life experience. In fact, education is a tool to help people to improve themselves or change their lives.

Take the time to think carefully of which degree you may need to help you to be able to achieve your life goal and future. To do this, you now have to fill in your goal in the table below. At every life step, bear in mind you do not necessarily have to fill in the stage which you have already passed (in terms of your age). See table below:

Stage: Year of age	Goal t achieve for Degree/Skills/Certificate	Institute and Venue	Score (you must come back to score yourself when you are reach to each stage) score from 0 to 10, 10 is very successful, and 0 is completely fail
A: 16			
B: 21			
C: 25			
D: 35			

E: 45			
F: 55			
G: 65			
H: 75			

Chapter 8

Work or Career Planning

Why do you do what you do, and does it provide you with everything you want? What do you really want to do? What choices do you have? The author will show you how to get the career you desire and identify what is important to you. This book will also will help you to set the right goals for your life, help you to improve your development skills and deal with work-related problems.

Work is a physical or mental effort or activity directed toward the production or accomplishment of something, something that one is doing, making or performing, especially an occupation or undertaking a duty or task. In fact, psychic people say that work can be done on an object when you transfer energy to that object. When you put energy into an object, then you do work on that object, in a short: work is the transfer of energy.

Work usually means the end product because it is only the component of the force along the direction of motion of the object. Career planning involves short and long term career goals, personal goals and constraints. It is good idea to have a short and long term career plan, which takes into account your career needs within the next five or ten years as long term.

You have to think about your career, you need to look at your career needs. This plan should be reviewed every year or so to take account of factors relating to your job and your personal circumstances, such as what you want to be doing in your job. Perhaps in higher positions, higher grades of management and developing specialist knowledge, teaching or training other people about your job. What working conditions do you want? Perhaps more or less travel, regular working hours, scope to use your languages or other specialist skills, timing, family factors, or planning for retirement.

If you are looking to change career direction or if you are going to graduate or you are contemplating a career move that will take you back to the level of a new graduate entrant, then use the basic information about the profession you are considering, followed by making a proper plan, and discuss it with someone. However, before you can formulate a plan you need to look back at the information you have gathered about yourself, your talents, skills, knowledge and constraints, interests and values, your chosen occupation entry requirements, skills required, and if more training is needed.

Now you need to put together the information you have gathered about yourself and the career area. Can you meet the requirements of the job? Will the career you are considering meet your needs? Look at the possibility and significant implications. Go back and look at your career needs and ensure that all your requirements can be met. Try to formulate a plan that includes at least one contingency career area. Discuss your plans with your family members or other people who will give you objective views of the realism and practicalities. Satisfy yourself before proceeding with a career change or making a plan.

Career management is the lifelong process of investing resources to achieve your career goals, and a continuing process that is a necessity for adapting to the changing demands of the 21st century's economy. You have probably heard the term 'career management'; in the future, you need to be responsible for your own career. What you may not have been told is what career management is and how you do it. In fact, career management uses the same concepts similar to good financial plan. A good rule of thumb to keep in mind is a disciplined investment, a focus on two key investment assets to manage throughout your working years and your personal lifelong learning.

It is often surprising to realise how much of your day-to-day work is now based around technology. Computers and other scientific advantages have radically altered the way in which you conduct your work. Even more amazing is the realisation that there are more scientists alive today than ever before and the project rate of change will increase tenfold in your children's lifetime. The ramifications of these advancements and innovations will ripple swiftly through the economy, obstructing many businesses and catapulting others into the limelight.

How well you are able to adapt to these ongoing innovations will be directly related to how up to date you keep your knowledge and skills. Consider how to vary your investments in time, energy and resources. For example, topical certificate courses, or keeping your professional reading current, you have moved to an information and service economy and relationships have become an increasingly critical asset.

Clearly, today's tasks are with colleagues, vendors, customers and competitors. These relationships will be the source of information about how fields and industries are evolving; you also have relationships outside of these environments that may be affiliated with your hobbies, children and spiritual or community networks.

In reality, your personal and professional relationships will transcend specific companies, industries and communities. These will have an impact on your present performance and future opportunities. The truth is most people accomplish very little in isolation. "Networking uncovers more than 70% of your current job openings" (Miller, 2004). To keep connected and knowing how to build relationships has more impact than ever before. These skills can be developed in applied communication courses, effective listening and the genuine desire to get to know people better.

Life planning and career management form the backdrop of successful career management. Creating a vision and plan are also essential to guiding informed investment decisions and establishing short and long term goals. The career plan you established should be broad enough to be flexible, but specific enough to be actionable.

The career plan should build on a profile of your unique traits, direct your choices to develop what you need to be satisfied, and be able to successfully contribute in different work environments over many years of your whole lifetime. To maintain your adaptability and employability, habitually establishing life learning goals and nurturing your relationships are the keys to productive career management.

The reality is you never stop learning; you should never be in a place where you think you know it all. Once you figure out what it is you are going to start reading and learning more about in that specific niche, keep up to date with changing trends. Things change every day; if you are constantly educating yourself you should be able to predict when certain changes will occur and you will be able to change along with it. The only way to keep growing is to keep learning.

There is a pneumonic that you may have to be aware of: 'FOCUS', the author breaks it down to: F is follow, O is one, C is concentration, U is until and S is successful. So the most appropriate technique for everyone to succeed in anything is to follow your plan and goal and only one goal at a time. "Concentrate on what you are doing, or what are you going to do, and stay focused, keep trying, working harder than ever until you are successful in your goals or plan" (Miller, 2004).

Career is very important because employers look for more than a degree and work experience; they look to see if you can give that extra edge. It helps you develop understanding of the world of work and awareness of your own skills and abilities. The experience may also help you get your first graduate job, as some employers use the vacations and longer placements to identify their future workforce. All work experience is valuable as long as you learn something from it. To get the most out of the experience, it is worth taking some time to consider the type of experience you wish to gain and what you want from your working life.

You can learn from experiences in the world of work. Work experience allows theory and practice to be closely linked. This relationship is essential to higher education especially in engineering, business and vocational areas such as hospitality. However, you can use your work experience to build on your strengths or work on your weaknesses. Understanding your strategies, skills, and interests can be a good starting point of deciding what kind of work experience is best for you.

Getting a good degree is obvious, but being able to demonstrate to an employer that you have a wide variety of other skills will improve your employment prospects. Plan now so you can build on these skills. The author knows that everyone at work today faces new and seemingly ever greater challenges. Developing the ability to adapt and cope with these unrelenting changes comes from really knowing your strengths, preferences, drives and motivations, where the qualities can be applied and you can decide what you want from your work and career.

Here is something to help you; for every background and age who is seriously interested in analysing your current situation with total honesty and confidentially, with non-judgemental objectives from a highly qualified professional. The author's concern is to help you at any stage of your career to make the right decisions now and for the future, from secondary school through to retirement.

Here is a comprehensive range of carefully tailored progress to cover your specific situation and circumstances, wherever you may be in your career and life path.

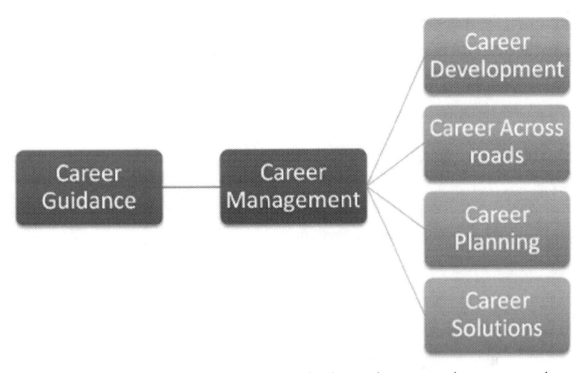

Career planning is very important because you need to know who you are, what your strengths are and what you enjoy before going to school, college, university or work. Even before you choose an alternative path in life, you should make the right choice of study, and the right work in order to become successfully employed or self employed in the right career for you.

Many people still believe that college or university is the only place for you to find yourself, through the experience of college or university life. In reality, if you have had no chance of having been to university in the past, the truth is learning does not necessarily mean only learning in formal institutions. You can learn directly from life experience; learn from reading by yourself, learn from listening, learn from other people's experiences, from television, radio, learn from so many media out there in order to have big successes. "As long as you have a clear goal and passion, and really work hard to get it, then nothing in this world would be able to stop you from being successful" (Glen, 2004).

Now is the time for you to think carefully, draw your plan and set goals to achieve in your life, in terms of work and career in the future.

Stage: year of age	Goal to Achieve for: Work For example, Role & Responsibility, Position	Goal for benefits you should have at work, for example, salary, car allowance, pension, bonuses	Score (you must come back when you are reach at each stage: score yourself by: 0 to 10: 10 is very successful and 0 is completely fail
A: 16			
B: 21			
C: 25			

D: 35			
E: 45			
F: 55			
G: 65			
H: 75			

Chapter 9

Finances/Money Planning

Financial planning becomes more and more important for most people around the world. For example, "More than a half of Americans, 55%, consider financial planning to be most important to them personally now than ever before" (Stephen, 2009). The growing importance of financial planning for most people is so important because those who plan accumulate less consumer debt and save more than those who do not. You will find out how to establish your value, take control of your finances, practical budgeting and how to set goals and achieve results in this area.

The question is: have you ever thought to yourself how much money you plan to save in your account for the future? Or that financial planning is only for those wealthy people with lots of income to spare? The reality is that a great salary with income to spare, does not guarantee financial success, nor does a modest salary necessarily preclude financial success. One of the most important steps in successful financial planning is just getting started. For most people, meeting financial goals and accumulating wealth requires time and planning. Regardless of your starting point, knowledge and wise decisions can greatly enhance your chances of achieving your financial goals.

Financial planning can help you make wiser decisions about saving for a home, education, or caring for ageing parents and can help you cope with major life changes such as marriage, divorce, birth of a child, changing jobs or retirement. The truth is financial information is so much better and more available today. The fact is, while being wealthy can open up opportunities that the less wealthy won't get, you won't get better advice by and large, which means that you still cannot outsource your financial life. Not only does the learning help you to avoid pitfalls that others fall into, the learning leverages all the money you will make in your career, giving you a double whammy as you career grows.

Money

Everyone uses money; we all want it, work for it and think about it. If you don't know what money is, you are not like most humans. However, the task of defining what money is, where it comes from and what it is worth belongs to those who dedicate themselves to the discipline of economics. While the creation and growth of money seems somewhat intangible, money is the way we get the things we need and want. The true story is that before the development of a medium of exchange, people would barter to obtain the goods and services they needed.

This is basically how it worked: two individuals each possessing a commodity the other wanted or needed would enter into an agreement to trade their goods. This early form of barter, however, does not provide the transferability and visibility that makes trading efficient. For instance, if you have cows but need bananas, you must find someone who not only has bananas but also the desire for meat. What if you find someone who has the need for meat but no bananas and can only offer you bunnies to your meat? He or she must find someone who has bananas and wants bunnies.

The lack of transferability of bartering for goods, as you can see, is tiring, confusing and inefficient, but that is not where the problems end. Even if you find someone with whom to trade meat for bananas, you may not think a bunch of them is worth a whole cow. You would then have to devise a way to divide your cow, and determine how many bananas you are willing to take for certain parts of your cow.

To solve these problems comes 'commodity money,' which is a kind of currency based on the value of an underlying commodity. Colonialists, for example, used beaver pelts and dried corn as currency for transactions. These kinds of commodities were chosen for a number of reasons. They were widely desired and therefore valuable, but they were also durable, portable and easily stored. Money is telling about an economy that is growing and is apparently doing a good job of producing other things, which are valuable to itself and to other economies.

Generally, the stronger the economy, the stronger its money will be perceived and sought after and vice versa. Remember, this perception although abstract, must somehow be backed by how well the economy can produce concentrated products and services that people want. That is why simply printing new money will not create wealth for a country.

Money is created by a kind of perpetual interaction between concentrated products, our intangible desire for them, and our abstract faith in what has value. Money is valuable because we want it, but we want it only because it can get us desired products or services.

Consider this sentence 'No money – No fun in life' the truth is, most fun takes place at sites which take you away from your work and you have to pay in money, travel and accommodation to have fun in external life. Now is the important moment, the moment of your life to make the decision then put it into a plan. How much money do you want to have in your life at different ages?

Take your time, think carefully, close your eyes and imagine. If you have the amount of the money that you want in your hand right now, how happy are you going to be? How happy are you for having that amount of money in your account? Please note: remember, think big, rather than small.

So the amount of money you plan to have, make it as much as you like, you are planning today. However, bear in mind the value of the money in whatever currency or country you are in, by the time you will want that money. The value might be lower than it is now. So please do think in the long term. For example, if you plan for the next ten years, then you must plan for the double value of what you have thought about right now. Now is the time for you to make a decision by filling in the following plan below.

Stage: year of age	Goal to achieve for Salary you plan to earn per month or year	Goal to Achieve for Monies in Saving Account you plan to have	Score You must come back to score yourself when you reach at each stage, from 10 to 0: 10 is very successful, and 0 is completely fail
A: 16			
B: 21			
C: 25			
D: 35			

E: 45			
F: 55			
G: 65			
H: 75			

Chapter 10

Life Skills

Henry (2009) defines life skills as having the ability to have adaptive and positive behaviour that enable individuals to deal effectively with the demands and challenges of everyday life. The UNICEF organisation suggests that behaviour is changeable and can be developed by approach to designation, in order to address a balance of three areas: knowledge, attitude and skills. "The risk is, behaviour is unlikely if knowledge, attitudes and skills-based competencies are not addressed" (Liz, 2009).

However, life skills are essentially those abilities that help promote mental well-being and competence in all people as they face the realities of life. The truth is life skills are generally applied in the context of work and social events. With skills for life, you must plan to improve the most important area of life skills, for example: literacy, numeracy and the English language.

In fact, skills for life is becoming more of a national issue, many countries try to put in place strategies to improve their country's people. For example, in the United Kingdom alone, the government plan to improve people's life skills which target 85% of the population by 2010 (Liz, 2009). However, there are some core strategies and techniques that the author would like to discuss further because they are absolutely essential to your life. There are 10 core important life skills and strategies, including techniques, to help you to develop those skills for your life:

1. Critical thinking or decision-making skills- For decision making, we need problem solving and information gathering skills. Every individual must also be skilled at evaluating the future consequences of their present actions, situation and future, as well as the actions of others. You need to be able to determine alternative solutions and to analyse the influence of your own values and the values of those around you.

2. Interpersonal/Communication skills, these include verbal and non-verbal communication, active listening, and the ability to express feelings and give feedback. Languages are very much important nowadays, especially the English language, because it is an international language. It does not matter where you are as long as you can speak English, you can communicate on this planet.

   The truth is you should speak more than two main languages, if you were not born in an English speaking country. Therefore, English should be compulsory as your first foreign language and certainly, you may need an extra language. Consider this fact, there are six countries that are the most powerful in the world right now and will be in the near future because of their natural assets, those are India, China, Brazil, Mexico, America and France (Stephen, 2009).

3. Problem solving and determining alternative solutions to problems. Use reflective thinking to judge the effectiveness of choices and analyse skills, regarding the influence of values and attitudes of self and others on motivation. Cooperation and teamwork helps to express respect for others' contributions and different styles. Assess one's abilities and contributions to the group. Say kind things, share ideas, accept differences, follow directions and stay on task regarding ideas.

4. Self-awareness, self-esteem and self-confidence are essential tools for understanding one's strengths and weaknesses. Consequently, the individual is able to discern available opportunities and prepare to face possible threats. This leads to the development of a social awareness of the concerns of one's family and society. Subsequently it is possible to identify problems that arise within both the family and society.

5. International relationship skills - with life skills, one is able to explore alternatives, weigh up pros and cons and make rational decisions in solving each problem or issue as it arises. It also entails being able to establish productive interpersonal relationships with others, life skills enable effective communication. By being able to differentiate between hearing and listening ensures that messages are transmitted accurately to avoid miscommunication and misinterpretations.

6. Be able to manage feelings, deal with frustration, grief and anxiety. Look for ways of coping with loss, abuse, and trauma.

7. Manage stress, positive thinking, time management, health issues, drug abuse awareness, good nutrition and the value of exercising and fitness.

8. Internet skills search, communicate to global networks, staying current keeps you up to date of any information or technologies.

9. Negotiation or refusal skills - learning how to negotiate and dealing with conflict resolution are assertiveness skills which you need for life.

10. Advocacy is about influencing and persuading skills. Since the world became one small community, networking and motivating skills are two of the most important skills you cannot live without.

In brief, the understanding that the life skills approach can be successful, if the following are undertaken together: the skills should be involved in a group of psychosocial and interpersonal skills which are interlinked with each other. For example, decision making is likely to involve creative and critical thinking components and values analysis.

Content will effectively influence behaviour, skills must be utilised in a particular content area, what are you making decisions about? Learning about decision making will be more meaningful if the content is relevant and remains constant. Methods and skills based education cannot occur when there is no interaction among participants.

It relies on groups of people to be effective. Interpersonal and psychosocial skills cannot be learned from sitting alone and reading a book. If this approach is to be successful, all the components, life skills, content and methods should be in place. The fact is this could effectively mean that life skills can be learnt through the use of certain methods and tools.

This chapter is going to look at how good you are at dealing with problems which may depend on what sort of problem you are dealing with. However, problems are a useful and necessary part of your development. They can reveal things that you may not otherwise see, which is why the author would like to explain that you must treat them as an essential and inevitable interruption in your life. Do not waste time keep asking 'why me?' it is more useful to ask how you can deal with them.

There is a certainty in knowing what comes next. Few individuals go through life always expecting the unexpected. Problems make you feel out of control, removing the comfort zone or predictability makes you feel like you are in freefall, with nothing to guarantee a smooth landing. When the discomfort factor becomes so great only then do you start questioning and searching for new options.

There are some techniques which will help you get through and get over it. These techniques are building blocks. You experience problems on a very personal level, so you have to give yourself permission to think about a problem and experience the emotions related to it. Staying positive is not a process of denying how you truly feel.

By trusting your instincts, your emotions can become a safety net. They can work for you, problems can and often do cause pain and there is a natural temptation to look for the magic, problem free formula. The aim is to re-route yourself when necessary and get back on track as quickly as possible.

Taking responsibility for a problem and the way in which you define a problem will obviously affect how you deal with it. Most people still find it hard to accept that life does not always go according to plan. Just because you have your own particular agenda, so does everyone else. Just as you are prone to changing your mind, so are others. What was once a shared goal may no longer remain one. The real solution is to take responsibility for your problems and do not resort to blaming other people.

After identifying a problem, it is easy to get caught up in what would be best described as the symptoms. If you overheard the focus of a problem from another person, even if they are the cause of it, you might end up by expecting them to deal with it. The real principle is your responsibility to deal with it by finding a solution to the problem, with it the solutions to dealing with the problem could be ineffective; therefore, a change of strategy is required.

The reality is, more than 97% of people always have an excuse: most of the 97% always say: 'my partner is not supportive, my boss treats me badly, and friends take advantage of me'. There are solutions to this problem; 1) Learn to be less critical of your partner, tell your partner how you feel, seek the support you need from others, not your partner. 2) Talk to your boss about how you feel, improve your performance at work, report to the superior boss. 3) Stop trying to please them.

Developing life skills is very important. They help adolescents translate knowledge, attitudes and values into healthy behaviour. This can be by acquiring the ability to reduce health risks and adopt healthy behaviour, which improves their lives in general, such as planning ahead, career planning, decision-making and forming positive relationships. However, the author hopes that by developing life skills planning, this will empower you to push to have a great future and success in life. Therefore, now is the time for you to think carefully, take your time, think it through, then start filling in the details of your life skills planning as shown below:

Stage: year of age	What skill do you plan to improve for life?	Score (you must come back to score yourself when you reach to each stage: score from 0 to 10: 10 is very successful, 0 is completely fail	Score You must come back to score yourself when you reach at each stage, from 10 to 0: 10 is very successful, and 0 is completely fail
A: 16			
B: 21			
C: 25			
D: 35			

E: 45			
F: 55			
G: 65			
H: 75			

Chapter 11

Family Relationships

Family is a social unit of people who either have lived or are living together, which can be defined as a primary social group, where both parents and children live together. An important difference among families is in the way that the central topic, the family, can be defined. There are four different meanings of the term family.

1. One is to look at families as based on structural features. Families contain a varying number of persons who are related in particular ways, including mothers, fathers and children. This view may be extended to include grandparents, in-laws, step-relations and perhaps even former relatives. Structural definitions of family focus are on the composition of its membership. They maybe indicate that family members are related by blood, marriage or some other legal bond such as adoption.

    Sharing a household may be another structural feature. Structural definitions of family can also mean the type of relationships that create social bonds between members. Important bonds are created by communication, power and affection as well as the daily work and leisure performed by family members. Scientists have observed how patterns of social interaction among the members are structured, and can specify the various rules and principles that families use to organise their activities.

    Family may be structured by such characteristics as gender, age, and generation, as well as their connections to the outside world. These structures also are useful for distinguishing families from other kinds of social groups and organisations. Plans for the family usually focus on some limited structural form. For example, you may apply this to married couples or to mothers and daughters. Sometimes plans compare different family structures. A plan might deal with how parent-child relationships differ with two parent families as compared to mother led families.

2. A second way is to look at families based on functional elements. Why do families exist in the first place? Every human society has families, so they must serve some generally recognised purpose or function. Most functional definitions of the family focus on the importance of human production and the necessity of nurturing dependent children for a relatively long period of time. Functional plans often address the structural variety of families, which ascertain how affective each structure is, in accomplishing the requisite

functions of those families. Families without that structure may be considered to be dysfunctional families.

3. A third meaning of family is based on interactional features, that is, it emphasises the repeatable process of social interaction within families. Such interaction may be patterned or structured, but the focus is on the ongoing activity within the family, often conducted jointly by the members or otherwise by a coordinated, family plan. This relies upon an interactional definition which includes concepts and variables describing what each participant is doing, how the members influence each other, and the quality of their relationships. From this perspective, a group not having any particular structure could be counted as a family. Any social group that acts like a family would qualify as being a social family exchange plan, who often adopts an interactional view of family relationships.

4. The forth meaning of a family plan is based on symbolic elements. Focus is on the meaning of family and is based on symbolic elements. Focus is on the meanings, perceptions and interpretations that people have about family experiences. Only by watching how a person communicates or uses dialogue to challenge and alter meaning, have social scientists come to understand what family is, often this expression is verbal. The symbols people use to create and recreate family go beyond spoken words.

However, other important symbols are non-verbal intonations, such as bodily gestures, practices of dress and grooming, written statements, visual images such as photographs and the practical arrangement and condition of possessions in the home. Family plans based on the symbolic perspective emphasise various languages used to communicate, as well as the many artefacts with symbolic meaning created by the family.

These four meanings of family and plans are not always used separately; two combinations are especially common. "A combined structural and functional perspective informs a structured functional plan" (Kingsbury and Scanzoni, 1993) however, each of the four meanings of family can be used alone.

Think back to the times when you sat down with your older relatives and they told you stories. What are your most favourite memories of these times? Share some of those stories with your own family, children, wife, husband, partner or any other members and encourage them to tell each other story.

This is something that will bring you back to the root of your family's relationship. What is it? It is a love from someone who is sincere to you from his or her heart. The truth is no one else in this world loves you as much as your mother or your father. The love your parents feel is love from their heart, which protects and looks after you. Some might argue that it is rare for parents in certain circumstances and within some families, not to show their kids how much they love them, but this not the case.

Most importantly, is the love you have deep in your heart which is the most valued of all things in your life. There is nothing that can compensate or compare with this value, such as money because without this love the author cannot see how you are going to continue living. However, you might be disappointed when you look at your life and say "No, I cannot see my family loving me." With positive thinking and a good attitude, you should think about this in another way. In fact, you are now reading this chapter, which is explaining to you what love is, how love is important, how much love is valued, love is such an important, magic word. You should know by now what it is, why you want it and that without love you cannot live. So if you have the answer that no one loves you, the fact is, you have love. You know what it means and how important it is to you to stay alive.

They are two ways how love impact on us. One is by taking the love from somebody, this is something you receive from someone, who is willing to give you their heart, which most people expect to have and have learned to take love from others. It is quite rare for people to be learning how to give love to others. However, please note, someone who is not from your own family is hardly going to be identified as being the true love by them.

And secondly, is the giving love to someone else. Because you know or have answered the above, then you have to learn how to give love to others. It doesn't matter what you are, who you are, what language you speak or where you live, as long as you live just to give love to them. It doesn't matter if you know them or not, because we all are human and expecting to gain love from someone. Learn to love someone who you know or don't know, is a beautiful thing, it is simple, easy and valuable just to give love to people. Forgive, listen and give people a chance, be friendly to everyone that is a kind of love you can do, the love you give to people costs nothing. On the other hand, the love you receive from people should be valued and costs you as much as being alive.

However, now is the time for your moment of memories, you may remember this moment for your whole entire life. Think carefully, take your time, think through whom you are going to give love to, when, and how are you going to show them that you love them and care about them. First, start with your own family, as shown in the table below.

Stage: Year of Age	**Who** do you plan to give love to	**How** are you going to perform for your lover	**Score** You must come back to score yourself when you reach to each stage, score from 0 to 10: 10 is very successful, and 0 is completely fail
A: 16			

Stage: Year of Age	Who do you plan to give love to	How are you going to perform for your lover	Score You must come back to score yourself when you reach to each stage, score from 0 to 10: 10 is very successful, and 0 is completely fail
B: 21			
C: 25			
D: 35			
E: 45			

F: 55			
G: 65			
H: 75			

Chapter 12

Spiritual / Religious Life

Spiritual or religious life is about believing in something which is difficult to identify or to believe. It is something about what you believe in. It is something about your own destiny, about the controlling of your future and freedom to enjoy life on your own terms. It doesn't matters what you do for a living or how old you are, where you live, or even what your current training or education is, because the author is going to show you one of the most powerful ways that you can use to attract life's success starting today.

The author knows it works, because the author has used it for many years. Religion is something in a person or community which is seen 'from inside', e.g. by that very person or community. It is something necessary which can mould people's characters. In fact, it is like an internal life which is all things necessary. It's about constantly developing your soul, more so that you can call on the intellectual, scientific, artistic or literate life.

The spiritual or religious life is lived in, in depth. Of the soul, it is the life of the whole man; your intellectual life would gain immeasurably by appreciating this and would receive an inestimable advantage because of it, instead of attempting to supplement the spiritual life.

It should be recognising its necessity and importance, and welcoming its benefits and influence, the influence of how to live a life. How deeply important this subject is may be seen, in the varied words which people have used intellectuality and spirituality, and it is important to all of us not only as individuals, but also in our social relationships. For it is evident that we can exert no real or profound influence upon our fellow men, unless we live a truly interior life.

Clearly, these lives are essentially connected with that of the nature of our interior life; for our interior life is actually nothing more than knowledge of the truth and love of the good; or better, a knowledge and love of God.

The future life which is designed by yourself from your beliefs is naturally occurring in your life. In reality, there is some contrast. Many people live nowadays not believing in things such as religion at all. This is something which affects us from outside of the body which we can call external life. However, many people have said that they do not have belief in such things, but the truth is that at some point, they might ask for some help from the angels whom they do not really know anything about.

The truth is, spiritualism or religion is something you were given since you were born, and either directly from the person who gave birth to you or someone who has been taking care of you since you were born. It is something that the first people to look after you have been putting into your heart, your memory, your brain, especially in your mind – beliefs in God or spiritualism.

Spiritualism or religion is partly about respecting others, where people have their own way, own choice to believe or perform and there is a freedom for every life to believe or choose to believe. It is totally true that religion or belief in spirituality have moulded people which can come out as individual personal character from what they believe. For example, Muslim people, they do not eat pork and they are not allowed to drink alcohol. This affects their life socially, and becomes their nature or character of their life.

In this way, the whole of the spiritual organism develops simultaneously, though it may manifest its activity under various forms. And, from this point of view, since the infused contemplation of the mysteries of faith is an act of the gifts of the Holy Ghost, an act which disposes the soul to the beatific vision, must you not admit that such contemplation is the normal way of sanctity ?

The important question here is, without insisting further upon it; let the author now examine more closely the full development of your eternal life in heaven, in order that we may better appreciate the value of that sanctifying grace which is its beginning. In particular let you compare it with what would have been your beatitude and your reward if you had been created in a purely natural state.

If you had been created in a state of pure nature, with a spiritual and immortal soul, but without the life of grace, even then, your intellect would have been made for the knowledge of the True and your will for the love of the Good. Your end would have been to know God, the Sovereign Good, the author of our nature, and to love Him above all things.

But you should have your own choice of believing in whichever god you believe. Is god for you? Put simply, all religion or gods are all within you. The effective way of you believing in god is in your heart, destiny and spirit of life. In the same way as the greatest benefit you have, gained or received from yourself is to believe in god or to know destiny and they way of life, of how you are going to perform in the real world.

Whether you should have loved god or not, the author has no comment on this point of view, to pay respect to you as a reader that there is no such recommendation of what god you should have believed in. However, there is a freedom in this point, freedom for you to have your own choice to believe, which depends on your family, personality, society and community background. The author would like to comment that they are all very important for you regarding the spiritual or religious way of life and where possible impact both directly and indirectly in one way or another.

It is natural for a human being as to whether or not to believe in people's destiny. It can never feel safe, just as the eye never tires of contemplating the blue vault of heaven. Moreover, it is a spiritualism which is hard to explain, and therefore, helps you to have a good performance, as good as paying respect in your society.

There are generally many factors and concerns according to what religion people believe. The abstract of living a life sometimes may mediate impact in the human mind, especially as regards the mutual compatibility of the divine perfections. You should forever have remained at the stage of counting singly and enumerating these absolute perfections; you should forever have wondered how it was possible to reconcile the almighty goodness of God with His permission that evil should exist; an evil, too, which is sometimes so great as to disconcert the human mind. You should have asked yourself, moreover, how His infinite mercy could be truly consistent with His infinite justice. Even though we enjoyed this natural beatitude, you should still be urged to say: ' If only I could see this God, who is the source of all truth and goodness; if I could see Him as He sees Himself! '

What the most brilliant of human minds, what even the intelligence of the angels could never have discovered, divine Revelation has disclosed to us. Revelation tells us that our last end is essentially supernatural and that it consists in seeing God immediately, face to face, as He is: at source (God) has predestination (us) to be made conformable to the image of his Son; that he might be the firstborn among many brethren. Eye hath not seen, nor ear heard, neither hath it entered into the heart of man, what things God hath prepared for them that love him.

We are destined to see all the divine perfections concentrated and intimately united in their common source: Deity. We are destined to see how the tenderness Mercy and the most inexorable Justice proceed from the one Love which is infinitely generous and infinitely holy; how this Love, even in its freest choice, is identically one with pure Wisdom, how there is nothing in the divine Love which is not wise, nothing in the divine Wisdom which is not synonymous with Love.

We are destined to contemplate the eminent simplicity of God, His absolute purity and sanctity; to see the infinite fecundity of the divine nature in the procession of the Three Persons: to contemplate the eternal generation of the Word, the brightness of (the Father's) glory and the figure of his substance, to see the ineffable breathing of the Holy Spirit, the issue of the common Love of the Father and the Son, which unites them in the most complete outpouring of themselves. The Good tends naturally to diffuse itself, and the greater the Good the more abundant and intimate is it self-giving.

If such is the life of grace, if such is the spiritual organism of the infused virtues and the gifts, it is not surprising to find that the development of the interior life has often been compared to the three periods or stages of physical life: childhood, youth, and manhood. St. Thomas himself has indicated this analogy: and it is an analogy which is worth pursuing, particular attention being paid to the transition from one period to the other.

It is generally admitted that childhood lasts until the age of puberty, about fourteen, though early childhood or infancy, ceasing at the dawn of reason, about the age of seven. Youth or adolescence lasts from the age of fourteen to twenty. Then follows manhood, in which we may distinguish the period which precedes full maturity, about the age of thirty-five, and that which follows it, before the decline of old age sets in.

A man's mentality changes with the development of the organism: the activity of the child, it has been said, is not that of a man in miniature, or of a fatigued adult; the dominant element in childhood is different. The child has as yet no discernment, it is unable to organise in a rational manner; it follows the lead of the imagination and the impulses of sense. And even when its reason begins to awaken it still remains to a great extent dependent upon the senses. So, for example, a child asked mother one day: "What are you lecturing on this year?"

'On what man?' was the next inquiry. The child's intelligence was as yet unable to grasp the abstract and Universal idea of man. Most important to be noticed, for the purposes of this present subject, is the transition from childhood to adolescence and from youth to manhood. The period of puberty, which is the end of childhood, about the age of fourteen, is characterised by a transformation which is not only organic but also psychological, intellectual and moral.

The youth is no longer content to follow his imagination, as the child was; he begins to reflect on the things in human life, on the need to prepare himself for some career or occupation in the future. He has no longer the child's attitude towards family, social and religious matters; his moral personality begins to take shape and he acquires the sense of honour and of good repute. Or else, on the contrary, if he passes unsuccessfully through this difficult period, he deteriorates and follows evil courses.

The law of nature so ordains that the transition from childhood to youth must follow a normal development; otherwise the subject will assume a positive bias to evil, or else he will remain a half-wit, perhaps even a complete idiot, for the rest of his life. He who makes no progress loses ground.

This distinction between the three periods or stages of the spiritual life is clearly of great importance, as those who are charged with the direction of souls we all know. An old and experienced director who has himself reached the age of the perfect may have read but little of the writings of the mystics, and yet he will be able to answer well and readily the most delicate questions on the most sublime subjects. He will answer in the words of the Scriptures, perhaps by quoting a passage from the Gospel of the day, without even suspecting for a moment how truly profound his answers are.

On the other hand, a young and inexperienced priest, himself only at the age of a beginner, will have little more than a book-knowledge and a verbal acquaintance with the spiritual life.

We have seen that the transformation of the Apostles on the day of Pentecost was like a third conversion for them. There must be something similar in the life of every Christian, if he is to pass from the way of the proficient to that of the perfect.

Here, says St. John of the Cross, there must be a radical purgation of the spirit, just as there had to be a purgation of the senses in order to pass from the way of beginners to that of the proficient, commonly called the illuminative way. And just as the first conversion, by which we turn away from the world to begin to walk in the way of God, presupposes acts of faith, hope, charity and contrition, so it is also with the other two conversions. But here the acts of the theological virtues are much more profound: God, who makes us perform these acts, drives the furrow in our souls in the same direction, but much more deeply.

Let us see now 1) why this conversion is necessary for the proficient, (2) how God purifies the soul at this stage and (3) which are the fruits of this third conversion.

This is particularly apparent in the traditional distinction of the degrees of humility, which, by reason of the connection of the virtues among themselves, correspond to the degrees of charity. This traditional gradation in humility leads to perfection.

In the light of what has been said it will be easier for us now to describe the characteristics of the three ways, with special reference to the purgation or conversions which precede each of them. Purgation which is necessary even though the soul may not have fallen again into mortal sin, but remained always in the state of grace.

Religious plurality gave, and continues to give you a great freedom in the organisation of the many facets of your life: in education, marriage, family, profession and leisure including your social contacts. Religiously motivated social controls did not play in your own life, a significant role in case you had to make essential decisions. At the same time, please note that in these cases you had a substantial need to justify your decisions and actions both to yourself and to your associates (Example: care for ageing parents).

Religious plurality is experienced by some people as providing them with personal freedom and space for personal responsibility. But it also affects many people in less positive ways. The author will mention four examples:

1. Religious diversity can lead to religious indifference. In this case, one encounters an increasing indifference with regard to the question as to how one's own faith and other faiths are related to each other. They are not interested any longer in the questions of whether faiths or belief systems are compatible with each other, or if they are similar in some respects or mutually exclusive. This can be called an attitude of 'post-dialogue mentality' (in contradistinction to a pre-dialogue and anti-dialogue mentality).
2. Religious freedom can lead to a lack of religious orientation. This expresses itself in an increased request for religious counselling as well as the new quest for building up a religious identity.
3. Religious pluralism revitalises Christian confessionals. This is obvious when, for instance in church, members urge church authorities to examine the content of Christian preaching and teaching for heretical elements. Recently, disciplinary action has been requested in Basel against several church employees as a consequence of their involvement in esoteric and a religious dedication to the 'Black Madonna'.
4. Religious diversity provides fertile ground for religious fundamentalism. The latter is expressed as hate towards anything culturally or religiously alien and is manifested by the willingness to use psychological and physical violence.

7.   Effects of religious pluralism on professional life according to wide spread   p u b l i c opinion; the Christian mission has no role to play in a religiously   plural society and is incompatible with religious pluralism. The term 'mission' is, in this sense, equated with religious propaganda, with   proselytise, with an assault on the private sphere (religious 'breaking and entering'), with an absolutist attitude regarding the Christian   perception of truth, with intolerance towards people of other faiths,   atheists or agnostics. Based on such prejudice, the theory and   practice of missions are forced to operate   in a permanent apologetic posture.

> Paradoxically, there is, on the other hand, within the church, in the public and even in the academic field, substantial demand for musicological expertise to solve social conflicts which result from the coexistence with people of other faiths.

As a Christian theologian and musicologist, the author attempts to make clear that religious plurality cannot be viewed from a perspective above all religions, but rather must be seen from the standpoint of one specific perspective. In this case, that of the Christian faith - just as people of other faiths experience and define religious plurality from the angle of their own faith.

The author compares the Christian mission with the 'skin' of the church, and musicology with the 'skin' of systematic theology. Mission is situated at the extremities of the church, choosing the most possible direct contact with those faiths and world views which, according to their self-understanding, are situated outside Christianity or, at least outside the church. Musicology has to do with hermeneutics. It tries to explain the Christian faith for non-Christians and to communicate other faiths to Christians.

The purpose of musicology is to think about the relevance of other faiths to the Christian faith, but also to be clear about the differences between Christian faith and other faiths. To account for the Christian faith to people who do not (want to) belong to Christianity is the other task of mission and musicology.

8.   Religious diversity in my professional view

In addition to the question of a sustainable theology of religions, the coexistence of religious communities and individuals of differing faiths confronts our society with new challenging situations. Currently in Switzerland, people are concerned with several problems of religious law: separate cemeteries for religious minorities (Muslims); entitlement to construction of non-Christian assembly areas for worship (mosques with minarets; Hindu temples); questions of marriage, divorce and the right to the custody of children. Additional questions concern religious instruction in markedly mixed school classes.

Further issues are raised by religious and cultural problems of patients during hospital stays.

Conflicts arise at the intersections of cultures, and these occasionally result in violence. To give an example: Recently a teacher who championed integration of foreign students was shot by the father of a Muslim girl. But fortunately, in our civil society and in the churches and other religious communities of Switzerland, there is also evidence of a remarkable readiness to build bridges across religious and cultural gaps. Religions make people quite frustrated. People can be atheist, but at the same time, they believe in freedom of religion, as long as religions do not interfere in politics, education and health.

They should be separate from these things for they are based on beliefs and imagination, but not on facts. There are many indications that the combination of religious practice and stable marital relationships contributes to a strong and successful next generation. Many people already know that a stable marriage is associated with improved physical, intellectual, mental and emotional health of men, women and children, as well as equipping them with the values and habits that promote prosperous economic activity. Religious practice is also related to positive outcomes for the stability and quality of marriage and certainly people's lives.

In general, religious participation appears to foster an authoritative, warm, active and expressive style of parenting. In addition, parents who attend religious services are more likely to enjoy a better relationship with their children and are more likely to be involved with their children's education. Moreover, the greater a child's religious involvement, the more likely both the child and parent will agree about the quality of their relationship. The more similar their values will be and the greater their emotional closeness will be. However, some of the same research also shows that religious differences within families can detract from the parent–child relationship.

Stage: Year of Age	What Thing do you believe, and you want to improve	How Are you going to perform or practice	Score You must come back when you reach to each stage, score yourself from 0 to 10: 10 is very successful and 0 is completely fail
A: 16			
B: 21			
C: 25			

D: 35			
E: 45			
F: 55			
G: 65			
H: 75			

Chapter 13

Social Life /Friends

Social life is something you cannot live without; you might argue that you can live without society or being part of a community. This is depending on what age you are right now and what general experiences you have had. The truth is we are all a part of the world and living in the same community, in a society which surrounds us. The thing is that most people make and keep friends without really thinking about how they do it. Most people just pick up the skills automatically as they grow up. If someone has always been more of the shy, loner type then this person will probably appreciate some pointers.

It seems too obvious to write about people in society. There are those who can be quite negative and positive towards other people or society. There are some people who have always had a reason to not want to be friends or want to be friends with someone. If you listen to most parents and teachers, you will go to college believing that the only important thing for you to do is to study hard and get good grades. Nothing could be further from the truth. While studying and getting good grades is a good thing and will give you a slight advantage over other graduates, it is not sufficient to guarantee success in the workplace. There are a lot of other important skills that you need to learn to be successful.

Think about this, employers are looking for leaders, people who can make decisions, accept responsibility and give orders. But they also want people who are team players and who can take orders as well as follow directions. You might have heard of corporate politics. It is a reality in the workplace and you must have good people skills to survive the political infighting, this is a fact of life in most large and unfortunately most small companies.

The question is: Where do you learn these skills? Can you take a class in them? Not on any campuses in this country. You might learn these very important skills by developing a good social life while you are a student. Developing an active social life while you are in college is absolutely essential for learning all those important people skills that every employer is looking for in candidates. If you master these skills and have good grades, you have a bright future in front of you. But if you are not a student any longer or you have no college or university experience, it does not really matter. Because next we will take a look at how you can develop them that and discover a more important point of view.

This is something call social life, which now has a linked network, because you can create a network of friends that can last a life time and may someday be a boost to your career. After graduation, a holiday card with one of those 'happenings throughout the year' newsletters can help you keep in touch. Someday, you may be out of work and these people will be an excellent resource to provide insider information on jobs at their companies. Where do you meet these people? Almost everywhere, at sporting events, parties, social gatherings, concerts and plays, in the classroom, etc. In other words, you are talking about developing a network of friends with whom you share at least one common interest. Some of these friendships will last a lifetime.

Pretty much anyone can have a group of friends if they want to. However, you more or less need to have these broad factors in order. People who have trouble making friends often go wrong somewhere here: this one's obvious. The more rewarding you are to be around, the more easily you'll make friends. You can be far from perfect though. Even people who most of us would consider annoying often have a social network. Some people want a group of friends in theory, to ease their feelings of loneliness, but at the same time, they're a little indifferent to the concept. Some of us aren't as naturally social as others. When your whole heart isn't into the idea of having a group of friends, your efforts can stall out, or can be very start and stop in the process.

Get an Outside Life of Your Own

You don't have to be a hermit while you're pulling your new social life together. Go and see some live music, go check out the local bars and have a drink or two by yourself, go see some stand-up comedy, go to a sports bar and watch the game or start going to a rock climbing gym. Take some classes, if you're in college then join some associations and clubs, walk around interesting neighbourhoods and go to any interesting local events advertised in the paper. If you're going to read or play on your laptop you might as well go to a coffee shop to do it, etc., etc., etc.,

Doing these things will take the edge off any loneliness and boredom you may feel. They will also fill your head with knowledge of things to do and places to go when you are hanging around people. Also, just being in situations where there are people around, even if you're not interacting with them all that much, give you some of the feelings of having a social life. And through doing all these activities there are plenty of chances to actually meet people too.

This won't apply to people who have just moved to a new area and don't know anyone, but often you'll already have the seeds of a social life around you. You don't necessarily have to go out and meet ten strangers to have one. It's a lot easier to start turn existing contacts into fully-fledged friends than it is to meet new ones.

There are probably a handful of people you already know who could end up becoming part of a new social circle. The author suggests that you can probably think about people in this way:

Acquaintances you're friendly with when you run into each other, but whom you never see otherwise. People at work or in your classes who you get along with, friends of people you know whom you've gotten along with. Someone who has shown an interest in being your friend but you have never really took up the offer. People you very occasionally hang out with, who you could see more of. Friends you've gradually lost contact with who you could call up again. Siblings and relatives close to your age. Please note: you just have to take the step of doing more social activities with them than you usually do.

Meet Some New People

Getting more out of your current relationships can go a long way, but it doesn't always work. Sometimes you're at a point where you need to meet entirely new people. Not having easy access to potential new friends is a big barrier for many people in creating a social circle. You can go into more detail here: in short, the author would like to say that the easiest things to do are:

Meet one or two cool people and then get to know all their friends. If you hang out with 15 people, you shouldn't have to have met them all individually. Having a specific interest that you want to build your social circle around and then actively seeking out others who share it. This can be as simple as joining a team or club (which you'd want to do anyway, just to take part in your hobby). Being in a situation where there are lots of your peers and then getting to know some of them through your day-to-day interactions. Work and school are the two big ones.

Do Your Best to Accept Every Invitation

If someone invites you to do something, then you should go. Why turn down a free chance to get out there with people? If you're more of a shy or solitary person, it's easy to mull over the invitation and rationalise that it won't be that much fun and that you don't want to go. Ignore those thoughts and go anyway. You never can be sure how much fun something will be until you show up and see how it is for yourself.

Sometimes you'll have to inconvenience yourself for the sake of your social life. You may get invited to a movie you don't particularly want to see, or someone might call you up on Friday evening as you're about to go to bed, asking if you want to go out. Whenever you have two or more people in the equation, you're going to have to compromise sometimes. Again, just being out there outweighs these minor annoyances.

Invite Potential Friends to do Something with You

Ask the people you get along with to hang out. Give them a call, or ask them if you see them in person. Invite them to go out to do something really basic, like a coffee. This is the most important step in your life experience. You can meet all the people you want and they can think you're great, but if you don't take any action to do something with them in the future, then you won't form many new relationships. People will stay as the guy you talk to in class or the girl you chat to at work in the break room.

This is basic stuff, but lonely people often hit a wall here. There may be someone they joke around with at work, or chat to in one of their classes, but they won't take the step of inviting them out and taking the relationship to the next level.

If you hit it off with someone, get their contact information, and if you meet someone cool don't assume that you'll run into them again. Get their phone number or maybe their email address. If you're shy this may take a small amount of nerve the first few times, but it's one of those things that ceases to seem like a big deal at all once you're used it. You can also get used to the odd rejection quite quickly. Also, make sure people have your contact information in case they ever want to invite you along somewhere.

Have a basic grasp of how to make plans, depending on what works for you, you may want to do something one-on-one with someone or go out in a larger group. If you know a bunch of people and your potential new friend are going to do something anyway, you can also ask if you can go along.

Making plans can be tedious and unpredictable at times. Try your best to get used to it. It personally helps you to accept that this wasn't a situation where you could perfectly control and arrange everything ahead of time. You had to come to peace with the uncertainty of trying to organise something with one or more other people.

If inviting people out and arranging plans all seems like a big hassle, it also probably feels that way for them at times. They shouldn't always have to step up and organise things for you. Do some of the lifting yourself at times.

Don't be Picky About Who You Hang Out with at First

In fact, your initial goal is to just get some sort of social life going. So hang out with whomever you get along with and who seems interested in doing things with you. The first people you meet may not be100% your ideal friends. The benefits of just being out there as opposed to moping around at home outweigh this. At the very least, it's easier to make further friends when you've already got a few. Also, if you're forming your first-ever group of friends, you probably don't totally know what you like or want in other people. You have to see what different types of people are like in a friend capacity firsthand, and if you get along with them.

You should also give this advice to others, because lonely people tend to be more negative about people in general. Less naturally outgoing types can also be more picky about who they choose to spend their time with. If you naturally tend to be down on everyone you meet, you need to make an effort to consciously override these feelings. Plus, don't have an unrealistic self-image that demands you can only hang out with a certain calibre of people. Be realistic about yourself and your circumstances.

If you don't totally like yourself, you may also be averse to hanging around people who you see as too similar to yourself, as it can act as a mirror that reflects your shortcomings back at you. This may be justified if you have some irksome traits and understandably want to avoid other people who have them, but often you may be turning away legitimately good people who just happen to have some characteristics that hurt your pride a little.

As a general rule, if you more-or-less get along with someone, actually become friends with them first, and then decide if you want to be friends. If you're picky, you can come up with reasons not to befriend just about anyone ahead of time. But when you're already hanging out with someone, and you've skipped over your pickiness, you often find you like their company, even if they wouldn't have been good 'on paper' in your mind beforehand.

Don't Feel Making Friends is Super Tricky

If you're inexperienced with making friends, you may see the process as being more drawn-out and complex than it really is. Often all you have to do to make a friend is meet someone you naturally click with and hang around with them enough. You also don't have to know them for months before applying the 'friend' label to them. A characteristic of more social people is that they'll throw the word friend around pretty loosely when describing their relationships with people. But it almost becomes a self-fulfilling prophecy in a way. Sure, if you've just met someone it may not be a deep, intimate relationship but you can still hang out with them and have a good time.

If You Want a Social Life, You've Got to Make it Happen for Yourself

Being too passive is another big error. If you want to get a group of friends, assume you'll have to do all the work. Don't just wait around hoping someone will invite you out on the weekend. If you want to go out then get on the phone and organise something. Don't worry too much about seeming desperate or needy. Take the attitude that it's about you and you'll do what needs to be done to make some friends. Who cares if a handful of people think you're a bit too eager along the way if it all eventually works out?

Don't Take it Personally if People Seem Indifferent to You

Some people are often harmlessly thoughtless and preoccupied in the sense that they'd be happy if they hung out with you, but they wouldn't think to ask you themselves. Sometimes you have to take an interest in them before you appear on their radar. Similarly, some people are more lax and laidback than you'd like about returning your emails or calls. They're not consciously trying to reject you they're just a little more loose-goosy than most.

Be Persistent and Try Not to Get Discouraged by Setbacks Too Easily

Sometimes, you'll join a club or be introduced to your friend's friends, where you might hope to meet a bunch of great new people. Then you get there and the experience is disappointing. You may feel like you don't click with anyone, or you might feel like they're ignoring you in favour of making in-jokes with each other. Give these groups a few more tries, often you're limited in how much you'll connect with others on the first meeting. You may warm up to each other before long.

If someone refuses your invitation because they are busy or not sure if they can make it out at that time, then don't give up. Try again another time. Don't automatically jump to the conclusion that they hate you and you're fundamentally unlikeable. Assume the best. Also, even the act of making an invitation sends the message that you like someone and want to hang out with them. They may be unable to meet that one time, but now see you as someone they could possibly have fun with in the future.

When you meet potential friends, be realistic about your importance in their lives and how long it may take to become buddies with them. They probably already have a social circle and their world won't end if it doesn't work out with you. In this case, don't get too discouraged if they're not knocking down the door to hang out with you a day after you have met them. They may be busy and your plans may not pan out for another few weeks.

Sometimes it just won't work out with someone. You'll get along at the time, and they may express an interest in hanging out in the future, but for whatever reason things don't materialise. It happens to everyone and is nothing to get too down about. Keep the bigger picture in mind and continue meeting people.

Once You Know Some People, Build on This Foundation

Once you've made a regular friend or two, you've got a good base to work from. If you're not super social in nature, one or two good buddies may be all you need to be happy. At the very least, it should be enough to get rid of any desperate lonely feelings you may have.

Sooner or later, you'll end up meeting your friend's friends. If you hit it off with them then you can start hanging out with them as well. You can also become a member of the whole group with time. This is also a good reason not to be too picky about who you associate with. You may feel lukewarm about a particular person but find you really hit it off with the people in their social circle.

You can continue to meet entirely new people. Having friends will make this easier as they'll do things such as invite you to parties or keep you company in places where there are new people to potentially meet.

Maintain Your Friendships

Keep in regular touch with friends through the telephone, email, MSN, Face book, etc. Hang out with them on a regular basis. Every friend and acquaintance has a right amount of time you need to spend with them. Some relationships are more casual and you only hang out every month or less, other people will wonder if you've died if you they don't see you every week. Common sense will tell you what these amounts are.

Don't be needy and pester one friend too much. Don't rely on them to meet all your social and entertainment needs. You may not have a problem with meeting people and hanging around with them once or twice, but you may run into trouble in the long run. Don't fall out of touch with your new friends and acquaintances. Various traits can get to you at this stage:

You can feel insecure. You'll convince yourself your new friends don't really like you and drop contact with them in response to this imagined slight. Your lack of need to be social may cause you to not want to hang around with them as often, and you need to keep the friendship going. Shyness may make you too wimpy to call them up and make plans.

If you haven't talked to someone in a while, it's not really a big deal. You can still get back in touch and catch up. It's not even that awkward. Don't think you automatically have to throw the friendship away.

Be Patient

Building up a good social life takes time, so stick with it. It may take a while before you get a chance to meet some people you're compatible with. After that, it may be a few months before you're consistently hanging around with each other. It may be a year or more before you feel like you're really friends with them. It often takes time to go from having no plans, to having plans with the same person every third weekend, to having plans with a variety of people three times a week.

On the other hand, sometimes you can get a social life going quite quickly. Joining a club or team may give you an instant social circle. Also, if you're extremely outgoing, you can literally go out to some bars and just introduce yourself to people. Overall, don't get discouraged if things are a little slower than what feels ideal. However, now is the time for you to fill in the exercise in the table as detailed below;

Stage: Year of Age	Who Do you want to make friends to?	How Are you going to improve relationship and for your social friends (life)	Score You must come back when you reach to each stage, and score yourself from 0 to 10: 10 is very successful and 0 is completely fail
A: 16			
B: 21			

C: 25			
D: 35			
E: 45			
F: 55			

Stage: Year of Age	Who Do you want to make friends to?	How Are you going to improve relationship and for your social friends (life)	Score You must come back when you reach to each stage, and score yourself from 0 to 10: 10 is very successful and 0 is completely fail
G: 65			
H: 75			

Chapter 14

Asset Planning

Life assets are financial planning and wealth management, which should be one of your prime objectives. This plan can help you to take control of your financial and asset future. Whether you need life assets, to create life assets, manage life assets or enjoy your life assets.

With life assets the author recognises that each stage of your life journey requires different customised solutions.

These solutions are developed through the profession of which you build around your stage of life. Assets, in fact, can describe the management of assets that are invested on behalf of different sectors. "It is the process of managing money for individuals such as through stock, bonds and cash equivalents among others" (Andrew, 2009).

Most people should have a plan to own assets when they start getting older. This plan is actually a planning of your financial and investment for the future, so it might be a great idea to have some idea of what assets you want to own and apply yourself to planning this. Assets should refer to allocating which related amounts of various assets that you own. For example, if you own a house, a car, or have £14,000,000 with your employer, keep some cash in the bank. The asset should be allocated with the following values:

House: £2,000,000
Car: £45,000
Cash: £14,000,000
The total assets are equal to £16,045,000.

The fact that normally you should talk about asset allocation in terms of percentages of the total, as detailed below:

House: £ 2,000,000 / 16,045,000 X 100% = 12.45%
Car: £45,000/16,045,000 X 100% = 0.28 %
Cash: £ 14,000,000/16,045,000 X100% = 87.25%

The most important form of this example is the cash being saved in the bank is very high, up to 87.25%. This is how you can tell if you have very good financial management skills. The reality is that people should have at least 30% of the cash saved in their account (bank) as their assets. One of the key things is to discover about asset allocation with respect to your investment, there are different levels from general to specific. (Andrew, 2009), suggests that the best way to analyse your asset allocation is to look at your portfolio at each general level and then only worry about the specifics later on if you feel it is necessary. The main purposes of figuring out your asset allocation are;

Knowing what you have invested in. If you have 90 % cash and CDs, then your portfolio is very conservative and you are unlikely to lose much money. You are also very unlikely to make a lot of money. If this is not what you want then it is time to make some changes. Diversification, if you own a lot of different assets, then it is very hard to know what they all contain. By going through and figuring out what type of assets and investment you have put in, you can see how your portfolio is diversified.

Investment time horizon, if you have money in your investment account which is intended for retirement and that is many years away, then you can have a higher allocation to stock. If the money is for next year's vocation then it better to be in something very safe such as CDs.

This would help you to know how much control you have over your financial future. Many people think that the future is out of their hands because they cannot influence how stocks and shares perform or how fast the world economy grows. One guideline for asset allocation the author suggests is that you subtract your age from 100, to determine the percentage of your assets to invest in stocks.

So if you are 55 years old you would have 45% of your assets in stocks. That may be a good starting point, but it is recommended that you meet with a financial consultant for a personal evaluation to determine what may be right for you. Deciding how much to invest in stocks or shares is just the first step. Next, you need to choose which types of assets you want, which will help you work toward meeting your goals.

However, there are some suggestions from the many professional advisors from the world famous financial organisation, such as HSBC, Nationwide or Royal Bank of Scotland. They suggest that people should invest in their future with the home or housing as one of the best assets that they should be investing in for their own future.

This is because these assets give a high standard of return later. There are some figures that you can see: the housing prices are always rising. For example, they rose by2.45% in 2006, 2.33% in 2007 and 3% in 2008 (Phillip, 2009).

Now you will find it more difficult to make a decision in advance of what specific assets you are going to have in this section. This plan involves you planning for more than five years, perhaps your whole life. However you must decide which assets you are really going to have, that allow you to live your life and give you happiness. The decision clearly affects the goal set for this plan. You can hardly have a loving and supportive plan when you have committed. That is the only way you can achieve your goal as shown in the details below:

Stage: Year of Age	What Asset do you want to have (own)?	How Much value of the assets are you going to own?	Score You must come back to score yourself when you reach to each stage, score yourself from 0 to 10, 10 is very successful, and 0 is completely fail
A: 16			
B: 21			
C: 25			
D: 35			

Stage: Year of Age	What Asset do you want to have (own)?	How Much value of the assets are you going to own?	Score You must come back to score yourself when you reach to each stage, score yourself from 0 to 10, 10 is very successful, and 0 is completely fail
E: 45			
F: 55			
G: 65			
H: 75			

Chapter 15

Life Style

The power of life planning and opportunity lies in the incredible life style planning presentation, which does all the explaining of the fantastic plan and opportunity to change and improve your own quality of life.

The truth is that you should have your own life style and you need to clarify what you really mean by 'life style.' It is your desire to live as an upstanding member of the community, to be known a man of integrity. But amazingly, this is what got you rich, poor, well known, famous or a highly education person. So you will acknowledge that you are what you are, in some respects.

The idea of life illuminates these and many other fascinating issues in a new way of life. The roots are the freedom of what you can be and what you want to be is exactly the meaning of your own life. It provides so much valuable insight, close to a consistent understanding of life, in its wholeness including its natural, social and personal aspects.

The idea of life style planning is essentially based on the author's personal, scientific and real experience. He had the chance to enjoy the freedom and to see the differences in many different worlds, such as Asia, Europe, America and the Middle East. The author experienced with various theoretical models, trying to understand the nature of life, the society where you live and the future.

The life style is an increasingly popular alternative to traditional life style which, depending on where you are and what you are and what goal you have, is better and is of more quality and requires more discovery of international life style, rather than stay at home in the local traditional life style. The life style can be performed in different ways, relating to people's culture background, with individual families in a comfortable place financially and also relating to each individual characteristic in background.

Also, the time involved in recovery can be very short or long to get back to your normal activities in life. The life style has been performed in the way of individuals who have experienced some side effects. Actually, the life style treats some of the same symptoms of ageing as traditional life.

Life style is something you choose, the way of life, doing what you want to do. What activity do you want to do? Where do you want to go? What level of quality of life do you choose? The reality is, it has been named by generations of people who share the world, as a result of people's visions and experiences, and these have made generational differences which will have a larger or smaller amount of people in these groups.

Stage: Year of Age	What Life style do you want to have?	Score You must come back to score yourself when you reach to each stage, score yourself from 0 to 10: 10 is very successful, and 0 is completely fail
A: 16		
B: 21		
C: 25		
D: 35		

E: 45		
F: 55		
G: 65		
H: 75		

Chapter 16

Life Balance

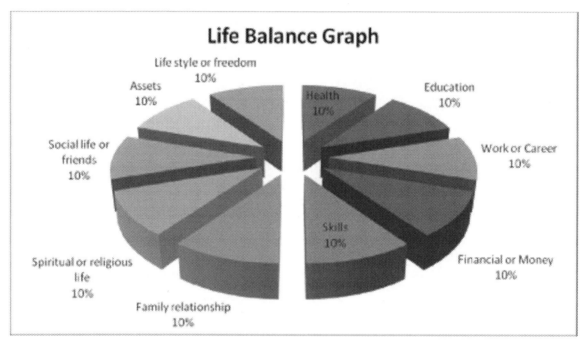

This graph is interactive, the 'graph of life.' The percentage of each goal of your life came from your score from the life goal table, which represents the different areas where you can devote time and energy in your life planning. Consider your level of satisfaction with each area, both time spent and quality. Please note how satisfied you are with your life balance and which areas need the most attention. You may want to focus on the areas where you are least satisfied or on areas that you anticipate will require significant change in the next few years.

Decision

Now is the time for you to fill in your 'Life Balance' table, time for decisions to be made. Now is the time for you to find out exactly what life you are dreaming of in this chapter, and then set it up as a life goal. Think carefully and honestly about where you are now in your life. Consider health, work, education, finances, family relationships, skills, social life, and life style or freedom, and anything else that's important to you. Write them down in each simple category, which are: quality rating of your life, scale of 1 through to 10, with 10 being the most important and 1 being the least important in your life, as per the table below:

Life Goal Table

No	Description	Score
1	Health	
2	Education	
3	Work/Career	
4	Finances/Money	
5	Skills	
6	Family Relationship	
7	Spiritual or religious life	
8	Social life/friends	
9	Assets	
10	Life style or freedom	
	Grand total	

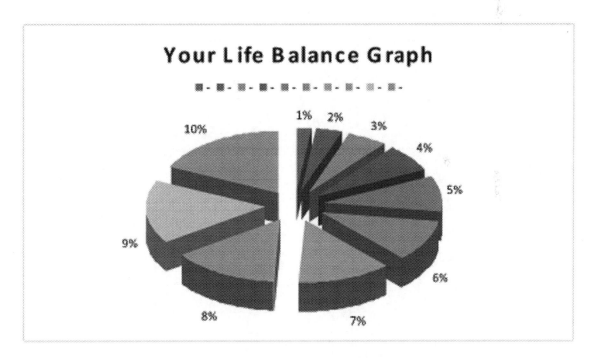

The author sincerely believes you are one of those people otherwise; you would not bother reading this book. So you are now walking into the door of success which is now open, and open wider than ever before. Put yourself on record now by writing what you are going to succeed in, you are going to join the 3% group who will get what they want from life. Now is the first step for you to take towards success. It is a basic step, it cannot be avoided, just believe in yourself, believe you can succeed.

In reality, there are only 3& of the population in any place, village, district, province, country and the world, who is successful. The other 97% are never or not successful in their life time. In fact, there is a name for these people, can you identify yourself of which side you are on? Please see and answer the questions in the table below:

Table 1: Successful signs

No	Questions	Answer
1	What time do you normally wake up every day?	
2	How do you normally control your spending?	
3	What kind of conversation do you normally have?	
4	How do you respond to your job?	
5	How do you respond to your family?	
6	Do you have a goal? How long ago did you set this up?	
7	What kind of food do you normally eat?	
8	How do you normally see things through, looking to the future?	
9	How often do you normally think to improve your life in terms of quality?	
10	What do you think you can do to change your attitude?	

Score: now is the time to score yourself which would help you to identify which side you are on, please answer the following details below:

Question No   Answer   Score

1 If you answer:
          Before 6 am   10 points
          Between 6.05 am – 7 am   8 points
          Between 7.05 am – 8 am   6 points
          After 8 am   0 points

2 If you answer saying:
          Always very careful, focus on value,   10 points
                    find out how to increase income
          Sometimes think about value, and   8 points
                    seriously think about how
                    to increase income
          Rarely think about value, and always happy   6 points
                    with the money you have earned now
          Never think about value; never think   0 points
                    about how to increase your earnings

Question No	Answer	Score

3 If you answer saying:

Always talk about positive qualities of your friends	10 points
Often talk about positive qualities of your friends	8 points
Sometimes talk about positive qualities of you friends; very often talk about negative qualities	6 points
Always talk about negative qualities of your friends	0 points

4 If you answer saying:

Always looks for more ways of helping others and looks for things to do	10 points
Often looks for more ways of helping others and looks for things to do	8 points
Sometimes looks for more ways and things to do, but quite rare to offer help to others	6 points
Looks for ways to avoid work, and not interested in helping others	0 points

5 If you answer saying:

Family is very valued, looks for ways to do things for family whenever you can	10 points
Love family, expects family to do things for you	8 points
Love family, but do not know what to do or do not bother to do things for family	6 points
Do not agree with those three answers above	0 points

6 If you answer saying:

Set up a goal longer than 10 years at a time	10 points
Set up a goal between 5 – 10 years at a time	8 points
Set up goal between 3-5 years at a time	6 points
Set up goal shorter than 3 years or no goal	0 points

7 If you answer saying:

Always looks for healthy food	10 points
Often looks for healthy food	8 points
Sometime looks for healthy food	6 points
Rarely looks for healthy food, or eats whatever you like	0 points

8 If you answer saying:

Seeing the future is a chance for you to make yourself successful and have unlimited achievements in the long term	10 points
Seeing the future is about planning ahead	8 points
The future is something we cannot be sure of	6 points
I have never seen myself tomorrow, I just make myself happy everyday	0 points

Question No	Answer	Score

9 If you answer saying:

Always look for more ways to improve quality of life as much as possible	10 points
Often look for more ways to improve quality of life	8 points
It depends on the circumstances	6 points
Not necessary the present is happy enough	0 points

10 If you answer saying:

Of course I believe everything could happen in this world	10 points
Yes I can do, but only something I am good at	6 points
No I cannot do that, because I am not good at anything	0 points

Now is the time to score yourself to see which side you could be on. However, if you score up to 80 points that means that the world should congratulate you, because you have got the ability of being on the side of the successful 3%. This is very different from the other people, do not be surprised if you are on this side, you need to get used to it. If you do not, then you might have to prepare yourself to face an unpleasant world, you are probably going to hear many people saying you are strange, some might say you are mad, doing something which is not the same as what everyone else does.

The author would like to warn you that this is the negative side, this is the disease to destroy you, to stop you from succeeding or achieving whatever you want to do or achieve. Be strong in yourself, believe in yourself that you can do, and remember no one else loves you more than you love yourself.

If you listen to the words of those people who can stop you going on to your goal, target or dream, I'm afraid to say that you are not going to achieve success in anything in your entire life. If you got a score less than 80 points the author is afraid to say that you are in the 97% side, you have done absolutely nothing wrong. You are doing things in your life which are the same as others' lives. For example, wake up after 7 am; eat what food you like, so this is something very usual which most people do. See the table below:

No	Questions	97%	3%
1	What time do you normally wake up every day?	Wake up after sunrise (mostly after 6am).	Always wake up early before sunrise, because you will have a longer day to do the work.
2	How do you normally have control on your spending?	Most people buy things they want without thinking of budget.	Always think reasonable quality and budget, look for more ways to increase income.

3	What kind of conversation do you normally have?	Always talk about the negative qualities of friends, or other people.	Talk about themselves and always positive qualities of friends or people, always motivate people's lives.
4	How do you respond in your job?	Looks for ways to avoid work.	Always look for more ways and things to do, especially helping others.
5	How do you respond to your family?	Think about themselves first, then the other after or might not think about someone else at all.	Always think about someone else, look for more ways and things to do for family members.
6	Do you have goal? How long has it been set up?	Sets low goals, short term, easy to give up when facing obstacle.	Set goal high- long term. Forward thinking, positive and high self motivation.
7	What kind of food do you normally eat?	It does not matter much what food you eat, as long as you enjoy it.	Always think first before eating any food, think healthy, plan to live a long life, life is always valued by doing things for people.
8	How you normally see things through, looking to the future?	Mostly see themselves in the short term, never thought about the life after retirement, just makes sure present life is happy and enjoyable.	See future as commitment and responsibility to someone else, family, villagers, friends, world population.
9	How often do you normally think to improve your life in terms of quality?	Rarely think of own life in terms of quality.	Always think and look for more ways to improve quality of life.
10	What do you think you can do to change your attitude?	Most people think of something that they might not be able to do. It will depend on different factors. In fact, this is 'cannot do' not a 'can do' attitude.	Always believe they can do whatever they want to do.

How Can You Improve Your Life?

How many times have you told yourself that you are going to improve your life, but ended up doing nothing? How many times have you been dissatisfied with some aspects of your life and vowed to change them, but did not follow through with your decision? What is holding you back, preventing you from improving your life? Is it lack of enthusiasm, motivation, desire, determination, will power and discipline?

Often, especially at the beginning of a new year, people make all kinds of promises to start making changes in their life. This also happens after reading a book or an article about someone who has attained success or transformed their life. However, the desire to make improvements does not last long, and the enthusiasm quickly wanes away. So is it really possible to be positive? Yes, but you have to have a plan, follow certain strategies and act in a certain way.

The author shows that there are some silent successes which should be able to help you to measure your current success, whether you are successful or not, and it may help you to be able to see which performances you may have to improve. There is one more question to ask yourself, when you think of success, do you think of: money, education, family, relationship or what?

There are many negative notions which are dangerous, because negative notions are pushing you to the negative side, which ultimately help you to fail at whatever you did. Do not pay attention to what those people are saying about you (negative). In fact, here are some basic facts that you should know about negative people. The behaviour and thoughts of those people are more predictable. How often do you have these similarities?

Please score yourself from 0 to 5 in table below.

Table A: Negative & Positive Successful Silence

No	Questions	Score
1	Feel sad most of the time	
2	Never have total satisfaction	
3	Put myself down, feel someone else is always better	
4	Complain all the time about headaches	
5	Don't like to live happily or don't have any time to do anything for myself	
6	Never achieve my goal	
7	Don't give myself the opportunity to succeed	
8	Don't take care of myself well enough, no exercise, not seriously eating healthy food	
9	I am young, still have plenty of possibilities and time, so I don't need to be in a hurry	
10	I am confident about my future success, I don't need to learn or list anything	
	Total Score	

5 = very often   4 = often   3 = sometimes   2 = rarely   1 = never

Table B: Negative & Positive Successful Silence

No	Questions	Score
1	I am confident in what I am doing	
2	I have good relationships with people	
3	I can get satisfaction in any circumstances	
4	I smile everyday	
5	I am a risk taker, willing to take the plunge	
6	Enjoy life no matter what the situation	
7	I can always produce the energy to easily accomplish tasks	
8	I can face all kinds of problems without too many difficulties	
9	I don't complain about my fate and life all the time	
10	I have to make sure that my dreams will come true	
	Total Score	

5 = very often   4 = often   3 = sometimes   2 = rarely   1 = never

Score Checking

You must put the total score of table B minus (-) by the total score of table A, in fact, table are the behaviours most negative people use, and table B are the positive behaviours.

More than 25

A score between 25-50 is absolutely good news. This means you are ready to be a successful person sooner or later. If you are not at the success stage yet, you might just need to have a look at what you dream is, and look at your strategies to make sure it is possible to achieve your goal. In your heart, you are absolutely a true fighter.

Less than 25

A score between 0-25 is very dangerous. If you are one of these people making such excuses, the author would like to suggest that you have to stop right now, you do not have to be smart or lucky to succeed, what you do need though is to keep trying. Yes, you do have what it takes to succeed because you are special. Remember failure is an embarrassment, but it is an opportunity to look for other ways and other techniques to get everything you ever wanted. It will of course take you some time to discover the principles to success.

The best technique is to commit yourself by implementing and repeating your goal and proven principles that have existed for a long time. Learn to know what to do to get back on your feet, even if life gets difficult for you. "The most important thing is to stay with motivation, confidence, belief and encourage yourself" (David, 2008).

If you start on your journey and are impatient to reach your destination, you will suffer and not enjoy the journey. When you get to your destination you will be tired and nervous, but if you focus on the path you pass through and on the scenery you see on your way, you will enjoy your trip and arrive fresh and happy. It is the same with all forms of inner growth. Focus on each step and don't be impatient to arrive at your destination.

Chapter 17

The Strategy to Make You Successful

A stable life is a representation of a successful person who has good health, a good education, a good job or career, good finances in terms of money, good personal life skills, good family relationships, good spiritual or religious life, good social life with friends, good assets, and more importantly a good life style or freedom for life.

It is a strategy developed by balancing values, and adapting to the principles of your own dream and planning for each important part where you can measure every stage of your life for every different age group. A strategy is the essential precondition to a whole life development programme of what is going to happen, when it is going to happen and how it is going to happen. These are experiences for your own life, at a certain age, aiming for your life goal. Deep and incredible impressions are performances, and eventually these impressions influence you as to a perception of plans as well as your own future actions. In essence, the development and strategy of life planning into your own life, is worthy of implementation and will give you a good quality of life.

This is a plan that happens and relegates the life to every untenable position in your life, the strategies being followed focus on your life stages while the plan works through to a world of success, happiness and certainty.

Consider, however, a life plan fully attended to and cared for by planning ahead, so make it a point to plan a quality life for your growing and learning needs. Family can sometimes play with you, support and motivate you and get behind you, attend your life events, treat you to fun-filled educational journeys, monitor your essential values of life, listen to what you say, guide you to what you do, introduce you to people in society and encourage you to have a successful life. In this solid life with exciting activities attached, it is not an exaggerated thought to anticipate the development of your life planning into a hopeful and well balanced person, always aware of your duties and obligations to yourself, to your family and to society.

Quite clearly, the author could be advised by the life planning of this incredible thought: "the character of a person is usually a reflection of your family life. It tells you how you were reached by your family and recognised by your family. If you never had it that good, very likely, you will have a hard time knowing who you are and where you will be." It may be a sweeping statement, but it bullets a very important point, the quality of life that you have affects the development of your individuality, and for this matter, the clarity and meaning of your future and life.

Randy (2009) suggests that there are six keys for people to have a successful life and future which follow:

1). GOAL SETTING, set clear goals to achieve what you want, do not underestimate what goal setting can do for you. The author hopes that you have done this from the previous chapter, according to each goal setting step, then you must paste it somewhere where you can see it often. Remember, your goals must be measurable, specific and have deadlines. Use your plan to help you grow and succeed. At every stage of your life, process your intentions, large and small, you talents, discoveries, your ten important plans which could make your life a success and certainly for a life of happiness.

"A goal is an objective, a purpose or goal is more than a dream. It is being clearly acted upon and it is a goal which you are working towards" (David, 1959). Making the right career choice now is one of the best techniques which can help and push you to higher success than ever before and with more satisfaction. Obviously, asking the question with imagination to be able to see yourself in the future is an amazing tool that you must have today.

This is your assured future. You should be explaining that this is your approach for you to select the right career; it is like going on the right journey with a clear direction.

The author believes the most important lesson in life planning is in the area of your chosen self. Before you start out, know where you want to go, and then you can work out the way of how you can get there, as early as you want.

To achieve the goals which you have created, you must make clear and use your talents, skills, abilities and demands. This could be the best technique so far and you can practice it, persuading yourself to become successful. Additionally, one of the best techniques which is suggested to you is to use imagination techniques to see yourself in ten years time from where you are now. Therefore, life planning can be the best personal guidance for your own life, which obviously is one of the easiest and the best strategies for people like you.

This serious life plan provides an important lesson, to be able to measure yourself in how successful you have been, how you are going to be successful and how far you need to go from where you are, both now and the future. In fact, this is one of the most important ways of predicting your future and your life, designed by your own life style.

The truth is that goals keep you feeling alive. The imagination strategy is a battery to push and motivate you, help you to work harder in order to achieve your goal. The good news is goals help you to live longer. There is no such medicine in this world, as the powerful bringing about of a long life and the desire to do something for yourself. The principles of life planning will absolutely work for you, only when you completely follow those principles properly with your self- motivation, persuasion and ambition.

Examine yourself and decide what specific things you should be doing to make yourself more effective. Use the form above as a tool to plan and head yourself toward a successful level in life. Then, when the lonely, lost, confused or empty return, check your progress and motivate yourself, stay focused on your goal or plan. This true life planning is the soundest investment you can make for yourself, but make sure you understand what life plans and goals in each of your plans really are. Often you measure a success level by the life line of the stage in life, or the number of successes that you have had in the previous stage, your health and fitness, degree, position at work, your finances, money you have saved, family- relationships with your family members, spiritual life, international life skills, assets and certainly the life style at each stage.

The key to your success is to recommit everyday to your goals, as consistent daily commitment is essential to your ultimate success.

2). THINK BIG

The magic of thinking big

Success means many powerful, positive things. It can mean personal prosperity, gaining administration, achieving leadership or being respected by your business associates.

Thinking Big

Before you set up your goal, the author has a great tip for you - think big rather than small. The success of people is not measured in inches or pounds, academic degrees or family background, Annie (2009) states that "the successes can be measured by the size of their thinking, however how big people think, determines the size of people's accomplishments." The question is: how could you possibly enlarge your thinking?

Do you ever ask yourself "What is your greatest weakness?" probably the greatest human weakness is self-deprecation which is an inferiority complex. Self deprecation shows through in countless ways. For example, if you see a job advertised in the paper. It is exactly what you would like, but you do nothing about it because you think, "I am not good enough for that job, so why bother?" Or it may be that Peter wants a date with Katie, but he doesn't phone her because he thinks she might turn him down, so what is the balance for this?

The fact is 'know yourself' which most people, it seems; interpret this suggestion to mean 'know only the negative self'. David (2004) states that most self evaluation consists of making long mental lists of one's faults, short comings and inadequacies. It is to say, however, that only you know your inabilities, for this example shows you the areas in which you can improve. If you only know your negative characteristics, your value then, is small.

There are some exercises to help you measure your true size of thinking which works. Write down the names of three people you know who have achieved substantial success. Write down the examples of assets frequently listed, which follows in this table below:

No	Assets	Person 1	Person 2	Person 3
1	Education			
2	Experience			
3	Technical skills			

4	Appearance			
5	Well – adjusted home life			
6	Attitudes			
7	Personality			
8	Initiative			

When you have completed this exercise, you will find that you outrank many successful people on at least one asset. Please note this will certainly work if you can be honest with yourself. You are bigger than you think if you're thinking to your true size.

The answer is you should think as big as you really are. The most important secret tool of this thinking is, think only in pictures or images, words are the raw materials of thought. When spoken or read, that amazing instrument, the mind, automatically converts words and phrases into mind pictures. In fact, each word, each phrase creates a slightly different mind picture. The mind pictures you see are modified by these kinds of words.

You are going to name and describe things. The point of this is big thinkers are specialist in creating positive, forward looking, and optimistic pictures both in their own minds and in the minds of others. Please note 'think big' you must use words and phrases which produce big, positive mental images. David (2004) suggests that there are five ways to help you to develop your thinking to become the big thinker:

1. Use big, positive, cheerful words and phrases to describe how you feel, when someone asks: how do you feel today? If you respond with 'I am tired, (have a headache, don't feel so good, perhaps it happened the other day but not now)'. This in fact makes you feel worse about yourself. The better response would be to say: 'Great' say you feel wonderful at every possible opportunity and you will begin to feel wonderful and bigger as well, then you become known as a person who always feels great. In fact you will win friends this way.
2. Use, bright, cheerful, favourable words and make sure you compliment someone who is an absent or third party, with big words and phrases. For example, 'he is excellent'. Sooner or later third parties hear what has been said, and as such, talk about you in a positive way.
3. Use positive language to encourage others. Compliment people's personalities at every opportunity. Have a special word for your wife or husband and every day notice the compliments that the people who work with you, praise and sincerely administer, have an effect as a success tool. Use it! Use it again and again.
4. Use positive words to outline plans to others, for example, 'Here is some good news' 'This is a brilliant time ...' 'You are incredible person'; 'You are excellent' people's minds will start to sparkle.

One of the truths is seeing objects or people and what it/he/she can be, not just what it he/she are, this is where mistakes are made, because people assume ideas with their previous experience or imagination (negative imagination).

There is a test to help you measure the size of your thinking, is your thinking big enough? To support your big thinking is significant; it is a positive vision in terms of your success including persuading yourself of your future life. You can motivate and lead your performance and activities by thinking big. You might need the next table to see how you can fit into the overall picture.

To assist you through this extensive resource, the author has demonstrated on the table below. This will then be compared to your real thinking and to see how you could possibly adjust your thinking, when the dreams and visions have been taken.

Situation	Small thinker	Big thinker
Expenses or Accounts	Figures out ways how to increase income through padding the expensive accounts.	Figures out ways to increase income by selling more products.
General conversation	Talk about negative qualities of his or her friends, the negative side of his or her company.	Talks about the positive qualities of friends, his or her company.
Future	Views the future as limited.	Sees the future as promising.
Work	Looks for ways to avoid work.	Looks for more ways and things to do, especially helping others.
Goal	Sets goals low.	Sets goals high.
Vision	Sees only for a limited way.	Sees through to the bright side, wide and unlimited in the long run.

Remember, the more you think big the more the chance for you to have a big success because you think big.

Example: This happened at Mercedes Benz show room in the city centre of London in 2008. An old gentleman walked in without an appointment, and asked for the best Mercedes Benz new model which was the highest price (£45,000) at the time. He was dressed in old clothes and carried an old bag; people could not see how it was possible for him to buy an expensive car.

Sale A: He saw him walk in, he ignored him, his mind was telling him that this gentlemen just walked in by mistake or he had no idea about the Mercedes Benz car. He then assumed that it was impossible for him to afford to buy such a type of an expensive car like the Benz. He then ignored him; he did not look at him at all.

Sales B: He saw him walk in, he then thought he did not look well dressed, but it did not matter to him, as long as he came in to this area it would be his responsibility to take care of him, no matter where people come from, no matter what colour they are or what language they speak. He then greeted him with a big smile followed by a warm greeting. ⊠He sounded like someone from Greece.⊠

He recognised his accent. The shock came just 10 minutes later when the gentlemen decided to buy the newest Mercedes Benz at £45,000 with his credit card.

This is something that can tell you that thinking big, thinking positive about people always has a positive return. In fact, this example is able to show the true size of people's thinking.

Here are some useful ideas that would help you to compare and recognise yourself and which side you are in. Please compare with the following table:

No	Question	Your answers
1	What time do you normally wake up every day?	
2	How do you normally control your spending?	
3	What kind of conversation do you normally have?	
4	How do you respond to your job?	
5	How do you respond to your family?	
6	Do you have a goal? How long has it been set up?	
7	What kind of food do you normally eat	
8	Do you normally see things through into the many years ahead?	
9	How often do you normally think to improve your life in terms of quality?	
10	What do you think you can do to change your attitude?	

Please note: dreams can be small or large. It will depend on your family issues, background, ethics, culture and experiences. The author agrees that these would have an impact on whether you will have large dreams or goals of success, as compared with a smaller scale. Here is an example, please consider this table below:

Dream Scale	10 Points	40 Points	60 Points	80 Points	100 Points	More than 100 Points
Compare salary of earnings to scale	£12,000 a year	£14,000 a year	£18,000 a year	£20,000 a year	£22,000 a year	More than £22,000 a year
You work very hard, you have well-matched skills and talents	100% 10 points £12,000	100% 40 points £14,000	100% 60 points £18,000	100% 80 points £20,000	100% 100 points £22,000	100% 150 points £30,000
You work very hard, but have no talents and skills are not matched	60% 6 points £7,200	60 % 24 points	60% 35 points	60% 40 points	60% 60 points	60% 90 points

You will walk like a swan which is straight forward; nothing else in this world can disturb or distract you from getting to the place where you want to go, as long as you know the direction of where you want to go. You should concentrate, stay focused and straight forward, there is nothing in this world that is going to stop you from achieving or being successful.

3) BELIEVE

Believe in yourself, you need to believe that it is possible for you to achieve it. If you do not believe in it you will never achieve it, when your beliefs are strong enough, you will do whatever it takes to achieve it, because for you, it is something true and you will do whatever it takes to make it come true.

Believe in something you believe in. You have to make sure that you really believe whatever you are going to do or be. This very important secret of success is to believe you can succeed. The fact is there is nothing magical or mystical about the power of belief. In reality, belief works this way, 'I am positive' and 'I can' attitude generates the power, skill and energy needed to succeed. When you believe, the power from your belief will generate the power to find the way and 'how-to-do-it' will automatically develop.

In the real world there are not many people who really believe they can do or they can succeed by themselves. The question you should be asking is 'how are you going-to-the top?' As soon as you start to believe you can do whatever you want to do, that is how the signal for life's success begins. It does not matter what you are going to do, big or small, it does not matter where you come from, where you live right now, what nationality you are, what language you speak, it does not matter how old you are, but all of these things are going to matter if you do not believe.

Belief is something you cannot buy from anywhere on this planet. It is a magic power and it is a bible for everyone's lives. Assuming you are now starting to believe in yourself, it is not just about benefitting only you; it will benefit everyone, everywhere, all the time. More importantly, believing you can succeed makes other people have confidence in you.

Belief triggers the power to do. Most of the time belief is doing much bigger things. The most essential element in fact, the essential element, is that believing in great results is the driving force. The power behind all great things in this world is the belief in success, which is one of the most basic, absolutely essential ingredients in successful people.

Look at it this way, belief is what regulates what we accomplish in life. Obviously, believe in yourself and good things do start happening. Your mind is a 'thought factory' to produce countless thoughts every hour. If you keep yourself busy in positive thought, being produced in your thought factory (which is under the charge of two foremen) is 'triumph' which in charge of manufacturing positive thought.

The other is 'defeat', defeat is tremendously efficient in transforming into action, but on the negative side, defeat is telling you how you cannot do, that you will fail and so on. What the author would like to suggest is that you must fire defeat, you do not need it around you, you do not want it around telling you 'you cannot', it won't help you get where you want to go, so boot it out.

All what you need to do is tell yourself that it is time to change yourself. Now is the time for you to begin a new life, now is the time to move on and to walk in the right direction. More importantly, now is the time to be alive. Indeed, all these are signs which point you to demand entry into the top level in every field.

People who have the superior ability to influence others can direct people to work, serve people in a leadership capacity and motivate people to success or to achieve higher in their life. The author is pleased to tell you that one of the most successful people on this planet now is you. The author sincerely believes you are one of those people; otherwise, you would not bother with this book.

So you are now walking in to the door of success, which is open, and open wider than ever before. Put yourself on record by writing down that you are going to join a successful group which will help you get what you want from life. Now is the first step towards success, it is a basic step and it cannot be avoided. Just believe in yourself, believe you can succeed.

4) ENTHUSIASM is the fourth key to your future; it may be the most important key of all. Without enthusiasm, the other five keys become virtually powerless. Enthusiasm is the energy, the fuel, the blazing fire that brings about a successful result. A famous business man once said that "nothing great ever happened without enthusiasm". If you want to accomplish great things; if you want to realise great goals, if you want to live a great life, you absolutely must possess enthusiasm for everything you do.

Because enthusiasm is so important to success, the difference between success and failure is often minute. Two people with virtually the same amount of skill and talent can differ vastly in the amount of success they achieve. This difference cannot be attributed to having more ability than the other person. In fact, in many cases, the more successful person actually has less ability. The different is in enthusiasm.

The difference between success and failure is what people call the 'slight edge'. The slight edge means that you do not have to be 10, 20 or 100 times better than the next person. You must simply be slightly better to achieve great success.

How you can take advantage of the slight edge is the key to enthusiasm. Enthusiasm is like a magnet. It attracts you to those things that you set out to achieve. It creates the conditions for a successful result. It enables you to take advantage of the opportunities as they present themselves.

Randy (2009) also suggests how people can develop the power of enthusiasm, there are three critical steps:

1. Interest, first, you must have a strong interest or curiosity in knowing about a specific subject. In other words, if you want to be enthusiastic with people, you must be interested in them. You must want to know about them. You must want to establish a relationship with them. If you want to be enthusiastic about your work, you must be interested in it. You must want to know everything there is about it when you are not in work. You must want to read about it, learn, learn and learn.
2. Knowledge, many people are interested in any number of subjects, but until they really learn about these things, they never develop the knowledge necessary to create enthusiasm. Action is the key to turning interest into knowledge. When you are interested in something, you must act on it to find out the knowledge that you are seeking. You build on the knowledge that you are seeking and as you build on the knowledge of the subject you interested in, this creates the condition for the third important step.
3. Belief, This is where you transform your knowledge from simple academic information and facts to emotional commitment. This is where true enthusiasm is created. It is not enough just to know everything about a subject, you must believe in it. The only way to believe something is to test your knowledge of that subject. By putting your knowledge to the test, you create belief in the validity and truth of that knowledge. This belief generates a strong emotional commitment, which fosters intense enthusiasm.

The problem is that most people wait to be enthusiastic about something. The reality is unfortunately, enthusiasm does not hit people, it must be created. People must take responsibility for creating this enthusiasm in their lives. It is only then that you can fulfil your dreams and truly accomplish your future.

5). PROBLEM SOLVING

This section is going to look at how good you are at dealing with problems, which may depend on what sort of problems you are dealing with. However, problems are a useful and necessary part of your development. They can reveal things that you may not otherwise see, which is why the author tries to explain that you must treat them as an essential and inevitable interruption in your life. Do not waste time asking 'why me?' it is more useful to ask how you can deal with them.

There is certainty in knowing what comes next. In reality, not many individuals go through life always expecting the unexpected. Problems make you feel out of control. Removing the comfort zone of predictability makes you feel like you are in freefall, with nothing to guarantee a smooth landing. When the discomfort factor becomes so great only then do you start questioning and searching for new options.

There are some techniques which will help you go through and get over this. These techniques are building blocks, you experience problems on a very personal level so you have to give yourself permission to think about problem, and experience the emotions related to it. Staying positive is not a process of denying how you truly feel. By trusting your instincts your emotions can become a safety net.

They can work for you. Problems can and often do cause pain, and there is a natural temptation to look for the magic, problem free formula. The aim is to re-route when necessary and get you back on track as quickly as possible.

Taking responsibility for a problem, is one of the best ways in which defining a problem, it will obviously affect how you deal with it. Most people still find it hard to accept that life does not always go according to plan. Just as you have your own particular agenda, so does everyone else. Just as you are prone to changing your mind, so are others. What was once a shared gaol may no longer remain one. The real solution is to take responsibility for your problems and not resort to blaming other people.

After identifying a problem, it's easy to get caught up in what would best be described as the systems. If you head over the focus of a problem to another person, even if they are the case of to deal with it, the real principle is how is your responsibility to deal by finding a solution to the problems with it the solutions to dealing with a problem become ineffective, a change of strategy is required.

From the 97% there are always excuses: most of the 97% of people always say 'my partner is not supportive, my boss treats me badly, and friends take advantage of me'. There is a solution. In fact, with problem solving techniques, first, learn to be less reliant on your partner, tell your partner how you feel, seek the support you need from others not your partner. Second, talk to your boss about how you feel, improve your performance at work, report to the superior boss, and third, stop trying to please them. These seem to work and help you to achieve anything you want.

6) PLANS

A very successful life has a fully developed life plan. The question is why shouldn't you apply the same strategy to your life? The author tries to make it easy to look at your own life and create or find your goal, which is the important part, set up a goal as a target to achieve in your life, and then make strategies and task lists for every part of your life.

This book is easy to read and helps you to create goals and strategies and tasks of thinking as a tool for your career and planning, these tools are able to help you to access your career and set career goals, based on character guidance and talent in each area of your life.

Finally, to help you to create an expectation of assets, owning a list allows you to build your own life, as a destiny to go and help you to build your confidence and image in a mirror so you can see yourself at every single important step of your own life, on your own way in your own life time. However, have you ever wanted to get your life together once and for all? Have you ever thought about creating a life plan? If you know where you are going, you are much more likely to get there.

This book is going to help you to create one, which focuses on every aspect of your life and offers tools and lots of help in creating goals, finding your talents, creating goals and strategies and task lists to make sure you stay on track and achieve all your dreams and goals in your life. This book is all about you. Use this book as your life plan to define where the life is going and how exactly you are going to succeed.

This book is going to help you to carefully plan out every aspect of your strategy and find ways to organise that information and motivate you to achieve the goals of your life. Great lives take strategy and long term focused effort. This book offers a way to develop your own life plan and you will define your value and long term vision of where you want to be in your future life.

Reading tip: our thinking can improve our world.

How many of us think of changing ourselves as a key to changing globally? How many of recognise thinking as being the key? What if each of us sharing the planet could examine our own thinking and thereby improve our decision making?

How Are You Going to Succeed in Your Life?

The most amazing mechanism in your body is your mind. The problem is the mind reflects what its environment feeds it, just as certainly as the body reflects the food you feed it. There are some questions you have to ask to help you to understand this. Have you ever thought what kind of person you would like to be, have you ever lived in some foreign country instead of where you were born? What kinds of food would you prefer? What kinds of work would you be doing? Of course, you probably do not find it easy to answer all these questions.

But most importantly, would you be a materially different person if you had grown up in a different country? Why is that? The answer is because you would have been influenced by a different environment, saying this you are a product of your environment. Environment shapes you, makes you think the way you do, more importantly is still an impact of the size of your thinking, your goals, your attitudes, and even your personality is formed by your environment.

The truth is if you associate with negative people that would make you think negatively. There are some famous words: if you associate with bad people, they would bring you to hell, if you associate with educated people it would bring you to a positive result.

There are some suggestions that the author would like to express in this book, which are: to have recognition of your success, the sad thing is, what we mostly learned when we were young was, you are foolish to be a dreamer, you have not got the money, you have not got the degree, you have not got the experience, you are short, you are black, you are Asian, you are white, you are too tall, you are too fat, you are too slim, you are disabled, you are not intelligent.

In fact, these are very dangerous thoughts which are killing your dream, stopping your dream, stopping your imagination, and finally, this will stop you becoming a successful person, or in other words, stop you being alive.

Those people, who were concerned with you in the past, try to block you. The majority of these people are convinced deep down inside that they have not got what it takes. It would be a shame if some of them might stop you from becoming a really successful person. In reality there are 97% of the current world's population, who are aimless, hoping opportunity will somehow, some day hit them in the face. Please note the 3% of successful people are: adults, with considerable, hope for success who prepare themselves. They work, they plan, which take time, might be a decade or so, but even when resistance begins to build up, finally success would come into your life.

In conclusion, all of us would like to be in the 3%. The one that finds greater success each year, but the truth is if you are still doing things in the same way as other people, then this is not much different from the other people in the world. Beyond that, you are not going to be a successful person on this planet.

Chapter 18

Life Line

Life line is a measuring parameter tool for the rest of your life which will enable you to measure your level of success, whether it is above or below the level you had planned. Achieving high-level success should actually require the support and the cooperation of others. To gain this support and cooperation of other requires self motivation. Success and the ability to lead others means getting yourself to do the things that you have planned.

The life line is a success-process producing principle explained in the previous plan. It is this valuable equipment which will help you to develop your own motivation capacity. At this point the author has created this life line as a master for his own life which he has used for half of his life. To use this life line effectively, you must stay with the rules or principles that help you to do things for yourself in an exclusive way.

Following these rules produces results. Putting them to use in everyday activities focuses on the plan and carries on following the goal that you want to achieve. Develop your power to self motivate; with this activity you should be performing in order to support your plan of success.

This life line procedure demonstrates your life, so ask yourself to explain your reason as to why you have or have not achieved at each stage. In this way it can help you to find out your obstacles and weaknesses. Once you begin using the power of imagination, you will see your future self at each stage, through to your retirement. About your future and life, the author cannot see why you should not get back to following your life line as a tool for your whole life plan, for your own safe and secure future.

This life line is actually a tool which will remind you whenever and wherever you want and need it to. Thinking about the goals set, for the dreams you have made to influence yourself, is an excellent rule to have at every stage. The life line processes the tool to measure how far into your success you are.

The first important factor is age. The younger you are the faster success will probably happen. However, it does not really matter. This means that if you decide to go along with your life plan, you will achieve success in life in ten or 20 years, even until retirement. When following a plan, you must take into account the fact that life sometimes fluctuates up or down during the journey of life. You have to consider how life has fluctuated throughout your life in the past, in order to understand how fluctuating it could be in the future.

This fluctuation will impact your life journey whether the plan takes a fixed or floating life journey. The truth is if you make plans when you are still young, you can get an extension to your life. Remember that you might know someone or have a family member who is still young. It you help them to make a plan, the only option he or she would have available to them, would be to succeed faster, younger and certainly at a higher level.

Stage A: 0- 16 years old

In particular the age of 16 is an important milestone; it is the first stage where you feel you are an adult. You can learn to drive, vote and have more freedom; in fact, this stage is the first step to go further in your life. By now you are probably starting to see the things that make a difference and they are not as simple as an age gap. Life experience, shared values and common beliefs are the cornerstones of good and solid relationships. In cases of high school aged kids discovering dreams or goals at an early stage, these ingredients are all too often missing. As we get to 45 or older, it seems to matter less, because our life experiences are more similar. When you are a teen still finding your voice in this world, finding out who you are and what you want to be is significantly empowering to you at that age.

Correspondingly, you probably feel the need to analyse yourself with interests in life activities like going out, meeting people, spending most of your time with your friends. You start to feel that parents should not need to know what you are going to do with your life; everything seems to be done for the first time at this stage. If you discover your dream, know what you want at this stage, perhaps you will succeed when you are at 25 or 30 years old.

Stage B: 17- 21 years old

The most important thing is to discuss this matter often and show an interest in what you doing with your life. Instruct yourself to consider where you want to draw the life line regarding your own private successes. Remind yourself that it is possible to succeed at anything you want. Each age is important but most important is this stage as the author mentioned. Because this is the year where people's core values about life should be looking towards success or achievement and whether or not they will be met. These are the years where you can measure your achievement, or process on the success lives.

Stage C: 21- 25 years old

In this stage is the benefit of increased life ability, the rate of increase in potential income is more as compared to an expert at an older age, say after 40 years old. There is more potential for an increase in salary which is also taken into consideration as a factor, so one can easily earn a top up income, to meet personal needs or take care of increased necessities from real life situations. In fact, by this stage you have probably achieved success in something in your life. By this stage perhaps you have started to purchase your first home, first car or other assets for your life.

Stage D: 26- 35 years old

There are life options such as re-planning. This is a possibility where the motivation and focus is low in the initial period and increases at a later stage. This actually coincides with an increase in energy for life, which is powerful for you. This could be ideal for the young or old planners who are climbing rungs professionally, but this is an option available to you (the planner who owns this book, because you see every stage). This stage is actually for serious thinking, you must at least focus on what success for life really is and what it means for the future.

Stage E: 36- 45 years old

It may seem worldly, mature or sophisticated to be a much older man or woman. In reality, you are robbing yourself of some much needed personal growth time. You should gain maturity by surrounding yourself with both older and younger people, you gain by living and learning for yourself. It helps you to provide a better life for yourself. It helps you to realise what sort of monitoring of life you should be doing at each stage.

Stage F: 46-55 years old

Your life is changing yet again. You are getting older. This is a major area of concern for both men and women over 50 seeking to become successful. Not least because life experience and knowledge proves that success only serves someone strong enough, who can focus on hope. The truth is that men and women have the ability to naturally convince themselves about their life fortune and that this is the perfectly time to be giving your energy to something new.

It is your time to check how successful you have been so far, it is time to go back to look at your dream when you were younger, in the past. If you didn't succeed, it does not matter now. This is a factor that most people forget to take into consideration, particularly when you are at this age and the assumption is that you are still alive. Forget the past, now is the time to look further ahead and make a life change today.

Stage G: 56 -65

You might feel old by now, but the truth is age does not matter. As long as you are alive, you can enjoy your life activities and more importantly still have things to do to keep yourself busy and carry on for the rest of your life. You still have things to achieve and goals to continue to succeed in.

Stage H: 66 -75

The author hopes you are not going to stop your life at this stage, there is no old or young. It is no different a year in age to any others because you know what your life is and what you have been through in the past. In fact, this is the best time for you in everything. It is time to look at what you have been achieved and what things you can still go on with.

Take a more detailed consideration of what stage you are at now by checking your age stage, which is important as it helps you to understand the stage of efficiency at which your life is performing. The tool measurement simply compares the age you are with the stage that has been used to generate that stage.

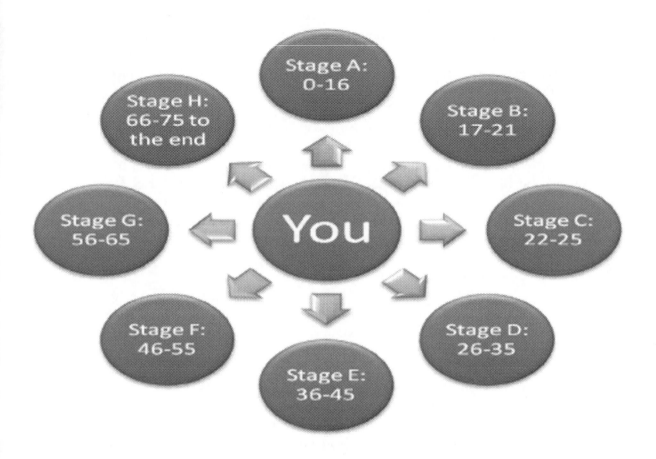

What Kind of Life Line do You Want?

Line A

The life line is a ladder programme which has been developed to address the new life targeting guidelines, to ensure that your life activities are being directed to the correct core of the plan of your life. The life line aims to be flexible and will address the specific needs of your life within your plan and support your plan improvement method.

Each stage of life should be focusing on goals and specific subjects. If there is an area that is not covered within this section of the plan, that you would like developed, please think about any alternative you can provide to support yourself in becoming successful in life.

Life begins with a first step, but then it progresses to a more vertical motion. Climbing the ladder of life, this is where life's ladder is extremely important. It is keeping track of all one's life, to climb one rung at a time. Step by step, reaching the goal, providing support rung by rung, whether made of wood or metal, ambition or soul, the ladder maintains through life's passage.

An assembled life line-type ladder was intended primarily as a life saving device for people who were actually looking for adventure in life, climbing rocks or mountains rather than living a very simple life, the same as all the others. The difference of this life line is a ladder step structure of your life from bottom to top and to the ends, joined at appropriate points by a plurality of perpendicular, the end of which is mostly ballasted at the bottom. The ladder is connected, from one stage to another, higher and higher along the journey of your life.

This life ladder is positioned from one stage to the next stage, preventing side to side movement so as to support the life balance of the ladder, thus maintaining the ladder in a strong position. In fact, this life ladder is leading you to expect a quality of life for the next stage, perhaps in five, ten or 20 years from now, certainly at a level higher than your current quality of life. Certainly, your future would be better than your present, otherwise it is a waste of your time to make a life plan.

In reality, this life ladder can also rate the present above the past, and the future above the present. However, taking into account all stage sets of quality, rating past, present and future, this seems to have adapted a method of introducing some of the life line in a modified form, which would influence you in your favour. Effort is reinforced through the influence of you actively learning at that time in your life. However, these may be these proud writings influenced by the author's life experience about experience in the 21st century.

The essence of the meaning of this life ladder has long since paved the way of life and is probably only clearly grasped in each stage of your life's success by a relatively limited number of weeks. Absolutely, the term has a special significance which the author tries to develop. Actually it applies to any stage combination together, having listed your life goal of strategies, each of them being responsible to the strategy directly above. The world's King of Pop, Michael Jackson, is an excellent example of high level world success.

Human life, even on this physical planet is only possible when it is organised using this model. The truth is human activities cannot function otherwise, and there is happiness, peace and harmony to the degree that you preserve various relationships without friction.

On the other hand, there is insecurity, confusion, unrest and social disease exactly in proportion as the links weaken or become ineffective. All these facts are so common that the deep significance is overlooked. Human beings direct their own lives along such plans because they cannot do otherwise. "Your minds are a part of your cosmic mind" (Paul, 2009), and you must follow nature's pattern or be torn to pieces. This is nothing that has to be learned any more than babies have to learn to breathe.

Gertrude (2009) comments that the ladder of life seriously employs what you can call the 'self-anchoring scale' on which you must first give a numerical rating to your present quality of life, then the past and future in the same way. The truth is it will most likely forecast the future personal progress including younger adults, and as you grow older, you should be expecting an improvement in the quality of life, which is considerably higher on the present ladder of life. Therefore, this type of life line is demonstrated as an adventure, exploring world wide experience and developing your own quality of life along life's journey. Now is your choice of which line you would like to have or to be.

Line A

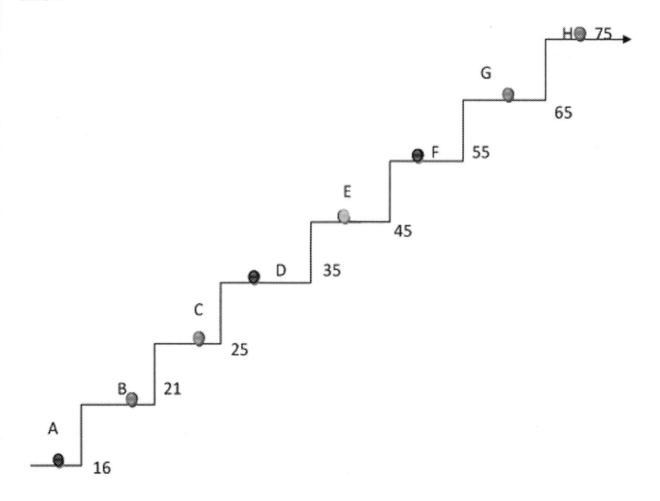

As you climb your ladder you will meet others on their way up or on their way down. Those on the way down find life too hard to handle and have gone to join the easy crowd at the bottom of the ladder, just milling around waiting for something or nothing to show up so they can grab it with minimum effort. The author suggests that this might not be you. You continue your upward climb taking those with you headed in the same direction and with your purpose in mind.

When is a good time to check your life progress? Of course, right now would be a good time and everyday thereafter if you are interested in improving your life. If not, you can just lie around and let the year creep up on you; it will be over before you know it.

But suppose that has happened. Suppose you are older now and have come to the realisation that you've missed the boat and let life rock away and you are still on the bottom rungs of the ladder, having made no significant progress.

Is it too late? Absolutely not, the good news is you can start where you are and with what you've got, even if it is nothing. You may be on the bottom of the heap, but you can start the forward motion.

All it takes is a little push, hopefully the author can provide that push for you as your personal motivation.

Sure, life is a tough, long haul, when you have climbed the enchanted rock. In reality the best technique is to keep asking yourself along the way, of where you are relative to where you should be? Where should you be at ages 16, 21, 25, 35, 45, 55, 65, and 75 or older?

How far should you go on this successful journey? Here is a great question for you. How tall should a tree grow? And the answer is, as tall as it wants to. Have you ever heard of a tree growing just half way and stopping?

Gertrude (2009) also suggests that there are some example excuses, 'I don't like it where I am,' 'I think I will stop growing,' 'I don't like the climate here so I will move to another state'. Have you ever imagined what would happen, if the climate is the same there? What then? What if the tree says 'I don't like the weather here'?

It is too hot, too cold, too wet or too dry. The question is do you know exactly what people do? Most of the people complain about the seasons of life when that is all they have. Sometimes you just have to put up with where you are at in life and get on with it. Stop complaining, it does not help you if nothing changes because of your complaints.

Line B

Straight life line

At this type of line perhaps you might be starting when you are at school. Everything is perfect, with parents there to help you. Progress happens in a line, for example, graduating with GCSE's at 16, you will go on to take A levels at college, and after three years at university, you will get a degree. You would automatically progress into work. The work system is a great security line which provides you with a very clear path and sense of direction, whereas life itself does not happen in a straight line, nor is it mapped out for you.

There are straight lines for work, no need to fight to survive, for example in these kinds of occupations: scientist, teacher, nurse or doctor. In fact, it depends, even in these occupations there are still ups and downs, highs and lows. It is up to each and every one of us to clear our own path through the forest and make our way through. If you think you are happy to be a teacher for now, but you want to get higher in your profession, then dream to be a head teacher in the next five years if you are not happy with being a teacher for your whole life. So your life line should be in this type of line in this case.

If you think you want to get to a higher level, then this should require you to take responsibility for yourself in every way. This is something that you have not necessarily been taught how to do and something that you often resist doing, because it makes you truly accountable for how you life turns out.

The fact that life is not really a straight line is also hugely exciting. It means that you can make it go in whichever direction you choose. It also means accepting that your destiny lies in your hands and you are shaping it each and everyday.

Rather than being subject to someone else's terms and conditions, you can create your own. It is, in fact, the ultimate freedom, one to be embraced with both hands.

In reality, everyone is taught that there is a right and wrong way to do things from their parents. Many people are afraid of making mistakes, of not getting it right. This paralyses people and people become afraid of moving forward in any direction. But it is an illusion, everything you do that helps you to learn and grow is what is right for you.

Those things are what will take you to the next level and ensure your success as a person. It will take you in a zigzag 'round about' manner, but that's fine because that's life and life is not a straight line.

However, perhaps many people like to have a straight line because there is no need for any suffering and fighting in life. There is one way or you might modify it, to use both ways of doing things and all people should be doing it that way.

Now it's time to listen to the little voice inside your head, to let common sense take hold of you. It's time to stop worrying about what other people think, and think about what you want and which choices you need to make.

The most basic rules of life are simple and straightforward. You are willing to give yourself that one chance to get you to a higher level, so which life ladder or life straight life line do you choose? Things can get pretty confusing. Getting into an organisation by life planning strategies is smooth if you plan and secure it properly.

It's your life and you get to make of it whatever you wish. It is simple and if you want it to be an upright ladder or straightforward, you will have to make up your mind to start moving in the direction you want to go, and stop waiting for your time or someone else to pave your path for you.

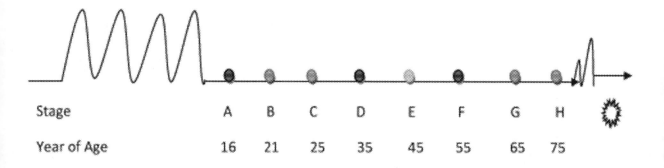

Stage	A	B	C	D	E	F	G	H	
Year of Age	16	21	25	35	45	55	65	75	

Life Success Measurement

A successful life is a measured by the accumulation of possessions and material wealth, which creates comfort in the quality of life. Consider the areas of health, education, good job and future career, earning good money, having good life skills, good relationships with family and friends, including good spiritual belief, assets and having a good life style in whatever style you like.

Shanelle (2005) suggests that it is possible to measure a successful life by power, popularity, control, achievement, winning and happiness. Having more and being more successful than other people is one of the measurement techniques.

In fact, a successful life is optimising the difference you can make in the world, for example, with your family, friends, community, work or church. The quality of relationships, the depth of character and the sincerity of your commitments can measure success.

No matter how attractive this view of success is, it has to be just in your view and be adaptable with your life's design. It should make you yearn for an ideal of love, truth, goodness and beauty that you cannot produce, and that others cannot produce for you. It could leave you open to disappointment, frustration, dashed romanticism and dashed idealism. It tempts you to think you can do it all yourselves.

The most important level of success counteracts these problems because it brings a universal perspective to the foreground. If you have faith, you might call it God's perspective. You can contribute by making a difference, stemming from a commitment to grow in faith. Your concern is with what has ultimate, unconditional and eternal significance, God and your will. This is only possible with God's grace to lead you to where you cannot go yourself.

To measure how successful you were in the past and in the present in your life, you must score yourself both in the past and present at each stage from 0 to 10 with the following details below:

Scoring Principle

10 = very successful	9 = successful	8 = quite successful
7 = successful in some part	6 = 50% successful	5= 40% successful
4 = average	3 = poor	2 = very poor 1 = cannot score

For the coming stage, you may fill or score what you expect to get. For example, if you are 25 years old now, then you must be able to measure your success in the past: stage A and B at 16 and between 17-21 years old, for health you might have been so happy and looking fit, then you should give yourself a 10. However, now you don't feel the same, perhaps a little bit overweight, then you might give yourself at the current stage C, a 7. But for the coming stage where you expect to get fitter and a better score, perhaps you expect to get a 10 again.

Life Success Parameter Table

Achievement Details	Stage A: 0-16	Stage B: 17-21	Stage C: 22-25	Stage D: 26-35	Stage E: 36-45	Stage F: 46-55	Stage G: 56-65	Stage H: 66-75
Health								
Education								
Work/Career								
Finances/Money								
Personal Skills								
Family Relationships								
Spiritual/ Religious Life								
Social Life/ Friends								
Assets								
Life Style/ Freedom								
Total								

In fact you can see at which stage you have had most success in the past, and ask yourself why? What happened? Why you have changed? Can you get back to where you were or get a better score?

So now is the time for you to make a plan. However, you can use your plan from the previous individual chapters into your whole plan, as a table which is going to be your life's designation. Bear in mind, at the end of each stage, you must measure how successful you will be when the time comes at the end of that stage and year of age, for example. If you are in stage B, the measurement which you can use when you are 21 years old are as detailed below;

Stage A: 0-16 years old

Achievement Details	Plan to achieve (This is a target where you should be scoring up to 10 for each target that you have made for the later measurement)	Score **You have to come back to this score when the time comes**
Health		
Education		
Work/Career		
Finances/Money		
Personal Skills		
Family Relationships		
Spiritual/Religious Life		
Social Life/Friends		
Assets		
Life Style/Freedom		
Total		

Stage C: 22-25 years old

Achievement Details	Plan to achieve (This is a target where you should be scoring up to 10 for each target you have made for the later measurement)	Score **You have to come back to this score when the time comes**
Health		
Education		
Work/Career		
Finances/Money		
Personal Skills		
Family Relationships		
Spiritual/Religious Life		
Social Life/Friends		
Assets		
Life Style/Freedom		
Total		

Stage D: 26-35 years old

Achievement Details	Plan to achieve (This is a target where you should be scoring up to 10 for each target you have made for the later measurement)	Score You have to come back to this score when the time comes
Health		
Education		
Work/Career		
Finances/Money		
Personal Skills		
Family Relationships		
Spiritual/Religious Life		
Social Life /Friends		
Assets		
Life Style/Freedom		
Total		

Stage E: 36-45 years old

Achievement Details	Plan to achieve (This is a target where you should be scoring up to 10 for each target you have made for the later measurement)	Score You have to come back to this score when the time comes
Health		
Education		
Work/Career		
Finances/Money		
Personal Skills		
Family Relationships		
Spiritual/Religious Life		
Social Life /Friends		
Assets		
Life Style/Freedom		
Total		

Stage F: 46-55 years old

Achievement Details	Plan to achieve (This is a target where you should be scoring up to 10 for each target you have made for the later measurement)	Score You have to come back to this score when the time comes
Health		
Education		
Work/Career		
Finances/Money		
Personal Skills		
Family Relationships		
Spiritual/Religious Life		
Social Life /Friends		
Assets		
Life Style/Freedom		
Total		

Stage G: 56-65 years old

Achievement Details	Plan to achieve (This is a target where you should be scoring up to 10 for each target you have made for the later measurement)	Score You have to come back to this score when the time comes
Health		
Education		
Work/Career		
Finances/Money		
Personal Skills		
Family Relationships		
Spiritual/Religious Life		
Social Life /Friends		
Assets		
Life Style/Freedom		
Total		

Stage H: 66-75 years old

Achievement Details	Plan to achieve (This is a target where you should be scoring up to 10 for each target you have made for the later measurement)	Score You have to come back to this score when the time comes
Health		
Education		
Work/Career		
Finances/Money		
Personal Skills		
Family Relationships		
Spiritual/Religious Life		
Social Life /Friends		
Assets		
Life Style/Freedom		
Total		

Then score how successful you are in each stage. Wherever you have arrived, score from 0 to 10 as in the following details below;

10 = very successful   9 = successful   8 = quite successful   7 = successful in some part
6 = 50 % successful   5= 40 % successful   4 = average   3 = poor   2 = very poor   1 = cannot score

Achievement	Stage A: 0-16	Stage B: 17-21	Stage C: 22-25	Stage D: 26-35	Stage E: 36-45	Stage F: 46-55	Stage G: 56-65	Stage H: 66 -75 up to the end
Health								
Education								
Work/Career								
Financial/Money								
Personal Skills								
Family Relationships								
Spiritual/Religious Life								
Social/Friends Life								
Assets								
Life style/Freedom								
Total								
Percentage % (total score divided by 100 X 100)								

You have now worked out you score, so go back to compare how successful you were in the past compared with following details:

Score	Scale	Result
1	= 0% -10 %	cannot describe
2	= 11% -20%	very poor
3	= 21% -30%	poor
4	= 22% -40%	average

5	= 41% -50%	40% successful
6	= 51% -60%	50% successful
7	= 61% -70%	successful in some part
8	= 71% -80%	quite successful
9	= 81% -90%	successful
10	= 91% -100%	very successful

Who are you? / Who am I?

Now you have completed the practical part, which will be able to tell you who you are, what you are, where you should be going from now on and how long it will take you to get there. All of these answers are clear and you could answer yourself. You have designed your own life plan of which kind of life you should be having for the future after today.

These help to reduce your confusion while you are on your way to becoming successful. You should concentrate, focus, be patient, work hard, and motivate yourself with your imagination of being successful in what you want to be or have and see how happy you will be.

Of course there are times when you might be able to face life's problems by using your internal resources which come from yourself. This might be because of your life experience or perhaps because of your confusion in life. External affects such as the environment are not possible for you to control, sometimes you can call these an external crisis, for example, an economic crisis or a natural storm.

More importantly coming from someone else, they can be effective. For example, listening to other negative ideas, be careful of this, it might kill you and totally destroy your dream and finally your life. Please note this is very dangerous, and unfortunately, in reality there are a lot of people in this group, telling you what they really think of what you dream, telling you not to do what you would like to do, telling you what is not good for you, because they might have no dream for themselves.

Remember everyone has a different life, it does not really matter what relationship they have with you, it does not matter who you are. You must not let them design your life because you must have your own life and way. To listen to people is not wrong, but you must only listen to someone who supports you in achieving what you want to be, not because of what they want you to be.

This is a positive affect for you, which the author would like to suggest that this is something you should be looking at. This is the kind of person you should be making friends with; keep in touch, stay close and have a good relationship with this person, because this person is one of your important keys to who will be persuading you to have great success, who will enjoy watching you grow and have a better life.

However, knowing where you are supposed to go and what you should be doing in every stage of your life is much safer, it is a very important life weapon, helping you to walk through the door of success in life is one of the most important keys in being successful in your life.

Secret & Future Life Predicting

80-100 %: Happiness and Future Life

If you got a score of up to 80% the author would suggest that you would have a wonderful and happy life, you have already done a great job, you have been working very hard, you have been through a very tough time and difficulties in the past, so by this point you have gone through all those stages.

You have adapted your talents, stayed focused, followed through your life strategies and you have done it successfully. The author hopes that the people from your own village, district, province, country, the world and finally everybody on this planet are proud of you.

50-70 %: Confusion

This means that you have done a wonderful job so far, however there is still a lot of work to be done; you should take more time to think through who you are, what you are and what you really want in your life. Perhaps you might change your mind; therefore you might have to go back to your plan, on any particular plan. For example, if you got a low score on the health plan then perhaps the goal you have set up is not quite what you really want yet.

The author suggests that you should think carefully and go back to where it was modified at some point, and you might find that it was not really what you want.

Please note, hopefully this is not going to happen very often because if you have changed or modified the plan many times before, it can be very difficult for you to be successful because you have lost your concentration or you have made yourself confused with the wrong decision you have made.

0-49 %: You are Not Yourself

The unfortunate thing is that you are living quite a dangerous life, you are taking a risk if you do not know yourself or who you are, what you are, what you want, where you want to go, what your life is for and why you are alive in this world. Sadly the world will not know your name. This is not a surprise because you do not know who you are; therefore there is no reason why someone else in this world should know your name.

However, there are some reasons which you could probably explain for not being successful at this stage. If you have faced confusion, which can possibly be happening to everyone at this stage, please note this is very important. Try not to let this happen very often, because you may not have the chance to succeed in anything in your whole life according to the time concerns.

One stage could take you at least five to ten years, so you must seriously think and make the right decision now. You can see how important it is for your goals and your life. Taking a wrong decision could lead you to have a terrible and miserable life for such a long time.

The author seriously hopes that this section will help you to wake up, from sleeping or walking in the darkness. Shake yourself, wake up and re-fresh yourself and now come back to where you are telling yourself. 'I am awake now'; 'I am going to be successful'. What you should be doing now is going back to the beginning of this book and re-reading again.

Go through, carefully reading and seriously consider each part of your plan, re-plan them again, especially on the first part in the goals and talents section. Go back to find out who you really are, what you are, what you want in life, what your life's for, and why you are alive. Repeat this important section where you really need to understand and make sure this time you really want that successful part in your life.

Chapter 19

Preparation for a Successful Life

Byron (2007) states that preparation is one of the most important elements to success which also has both the internal and external benefits of reduced stress on the journey to life's success (time concerns). The truth is people worldwide wish that they could be successful, or at the very least, be able to do something that they would like to do.

This is the phrase that the author would like to remind you of again: 'Do what you love to do and you will never work a day in your life'. In fact, without preparation the author cannot see how are you going do this.

Preparation for success enables you to take advantage of opportunities when they are available. You won't have to let the opportunity pass you by. This preparation may be in the form of higher education, specialised training in an area where you want employment, sufficient money in the bank to buy into a business, or it may be in the form of people partnerships that can help you attain a position that requires sponsors (David, 2008).

Shanelle (2005) also comments that preparation for success also means that you have a detailed action plan to accomplish what you want. This includes the basic goal setting exercise that denotes exactly what you want to achieve which you have already done, and when you want to reach the end result.

Goal planning removes the stress associated with 'flying by the seat of your pants' and not knowing exactly where you are going and what you have to do to get there.

Preparation for success means you are emotionally equipped with the right attitude, to see you through obstacles that you will no doubt encounter along the way. This means that you are prepared to meet each obstacle as no more than a necessary stepping stone, or that each obstacle encountered is just waiting for a solution to help you further your goal.

Preparation for success means that any failure you meet is seen as an opportunity to learn from mistakes. Remember that failure is your best teacher. These lessons learned would provide you with a clearer pathway to accomplish what you want.

Preparation for success also means that with every success will come to the desire to proceed further. You must prepare to define what ultimate success you want in any given area, and be prepared to look at new horizons.

Preparation for success may also mean that you will eventually encounter stress that is stress associated with too many demands on your physical or overall wellbeing. This level of success means that you will need to be prepared to step back, step away, or reduce your involvement. At this level of success, you may end up re-defining your next steps that will serve to bring you happiness and joy.

This could entail everything from retirement, to the selfless act of volunteering your knowledge to help others less fortunate. There is no better feeling than being able to help others overcome what you have, with the benefits of knowledge and experience.

There is a story from Shanelle (2005), an example story for you to consider, about the businessman who was at the pier of a small coastal Mexican Village, when a small boat with just one fisherman docked. Inside the small boat were several large Yellow Fin Tuna. The businessman complimented the Mexican on the quality of his fish and asked how long it took to catch them. The Mexican replied 'Only a little while.'

The businessman then asked why he did not stay out longer and catch more fish. The Mexican said he had enough to support his family's immediate needs. The businessman then asked, 'But what do you do with the rest of your time?' The Mexican fisherman said, 'I sleep late, fish a little, play with my children, take a siesta with my wife, Maria, stroll into the village each evening where I sip wine and play guitar with my amigos; I have a full busy life, senor.'

The business scoffed, 'I am a Harvard MBA and I could help you. You should spend more time fishing and with the proceeds buy a bigger boat. With the proceeds from the bigger boat, you could buy several boats; eventually you would have a fleet of fishing boats.'

'Instead of selling your catch to a middleman, you would sell directly to the processor and eventually open your own cannery. You would control the product, processing and distribution. You would need to leave this small coastal fishing village and move to Mexico City, then LA and eventually New York City where you would live.'

The fisherman asked, 'But senor, how long will this all take?' to which the businessman replied, '15 to 20 years', 'But what then, senor?' the businessman laughed and said, 'That's the best part. When the time is right, you would announce an IPO and sell your millions'. 'Millions, senor? Then what?'

The businessman said, 'Then you would retire. Move to a small coastal fishing village where you would sleep late, fish a little, play with your kids, take a siesta with your wife, stroll to the village in the evenings where you could sip wine and play your guitar with your amigos'. The fisherman, still smiling, looked up and said, 'Isn't that what I am doing right now?'

The fact is we all are living in a world in which being successful is everything. Success is measured by control, achievement and winning. Having more and being more is success. Success by the accumulation of wealth and by living a plush life, having a million dollars, and status as a powerful man, it seems right.

Shanelle (2005) argues that money never made a man happy yet, nor will it. In fact, the more a man has, the more he or she wants. Instead of filling a vacuum, it makes one. Wealth may momentarily help us to escape emptiness, it cannot cure it. The quality of life in fact depends on your character, and the sincerity of your commitments to you or your family.

It is worth and wise to plan for the future, yet, what sort of life do you want for future? You would take sufficient time to question what kind of life you want, for it to be happy and enjoyable. There are different forms of success, you can go on living for success that is self-serving, over concerned about money, health, power or popularity, then you will know how poor or successful you are.

One example is the queen spider. Before she can make a beautiful web as you see, imagine how many times she fell down from climbing to the top, her body suddenly dropping on the floor, hurting her so much.

But she did not stop trying. She did try again, again and again. She kept on doing it, again and again. The only web she made caused her to fall down around five to ten thousand times, and at last, she made it. It now looks like a beautiful web, large and so secure and safe for her babies.

From this story, we can learn that there is nothing you cannot do on this planet as long as you work out, work hard, never give up and try again and again. Finally, you could become a professional of whatever you are doing or in whatever you are going to do, fighting the problems you have faced, trying to make it happen, remember try again and again then again. It seems to be the only way that you can become you successful.

Also, remember, Rome was not built in a day; it took how many years to build. Years and years. Finally, when made, Rome became one of the most beautiful cities in the world.

This is the same thing, whatever you think or plan to do or to be, make your plans properly, do it now, work it out, go for it, try it, again and again, and you will surely be successful in whatever you want to be or achieve.

The author is hoping that you are going to be one of the world's most famous, successful people in the future.

Good luck..........

Chapter 20

Check list

A check list is obviously something simple that can be helpful to people in making sure that they have done everything they need to do. Check lists establish a higher standard of baseline performance. It strongly supports your plan, which provides two main benefits.

First, it helps you with memory recall, especially with mundane matters that are easily overlooked in the life plan which could be undergoing more drastic events. Second, the effect is to make explicit the minimum, expected steps in this complex process. A checklist is used as an aid to memory. Checklists are presented as lists in lower case, on the right hand side, at the end of this book. A small tick in the 'yes' or 'no' column is drawn in the box after the item has been completed.

Every life plan should have check list. The general purpose of this check list is to make sure that you keep track of everything in life that you want and to keep track of what has been done and what has not.

Obviously, you are constantly going to be updating your life planning checklist, as you make progress with more and more tasks being completed. With this checklist, you will not only make sure that you are able to get everything done, but you can save yourself time. To make your own checklist, all you need to do is to make a list of all the different tasks that you need to get done, in as best chronological order as you can.

Keep in mind that it really does not matter what order you do these tasks, at least for the most part and the most important thing is that you mark these tasks off as you get them done, so that you can keep track and make sure that everything gets done in the time of each and every life stage and age.

NO	QUESTIONS	YES	NO
1	Have you made a decision of which dream you want to make come true?		
2	Have you made sure you have only one dream?		
3	Have you discovered your talent?		

4	What talent have you got?		
5	Have you transformed (set up) your goals from your dream?		
6	Have you implemented your talents, which are strategies to follow, to help you to achieve your goal?		
7	Have you drawn your life tree? Which tree is yours?		
8	Have you chosen your life line? Which life line is yours?		
9	Have you measured your success from the previous stage? Did you succeed? What score have you got?		
10	Have you planned to succeed in the present? What score have you planned to achieve?		
11	Have you planned to succeed in the future? What score have you planned to achieve?		
12	Do you know of what the core of your life is (dream as a goal)?		
13	Do you know what to do to achieve your core (dream as a goal)?		
14	Do you know who you are?		
15	Do you know where you are going (direction)?		
16	Have you made sure that your goal is clear?		
17	Do you know how long you want to live your life (what stage)?		
18	Do you know what life style you want to have when you retire?		
19	Have you decided who you want to live with to the end of your life?		
20	Do you know who it is you love most?		
21	Have you done something special for him/her yet? Or do you plan to do something special for him/her?		
22	Who do you want to make proud of you, being a successful person?		
23	Who are you going to tell when you have succeeded?		
24	Have you planned to improve your health? What score would you like to have?		

NO	QUESTION	YES	NO
25	Have you planned to improve your education? What degree or professional certificate are you going to gain? What training are you going to take to help you to have a higher level of success? What experiences are you going to have to help you to become a professional in the occupation are you in?		
26	Have you planned to succeed with your finances (money)? How much money have you planned to earn? In each stage? How much money have you planned to have in your savings account? In each stage? How much money have you planned to earn for the future?		
27	Have you succeeded financially in the past? How much money have you made before? How much money have you saved in your savings account before?		
28	Have you planned to improve your relationships with family members? Mother, father, sister, brother, wife, husband, son, daughter and cousin?		
29	Have you planned to improve your religious beliefs? Have you read some good books to persuade your belief in religion?		
30	Have you planned to own some important assets? For example, lands, cars, businesses etc. If your answer is yes, what assets have you planned to own?		
31	Have you planned to improve your personal skills? Do you know which skills you might need to improve to help you succeed faster? Do you know where can you get help in terms of improving your skills?		
32	Have you planned to improve your social life? Who are going to be your best friends? Who are going to be your long term friends? Have you made friends in your neighbourhood? Do you have any strategy or technique to build relationships with new friends?		
33	Have you chosen which life style you want to have to make sure you are happy in your life?		

34	Have you chosen where you are going to settle down in your life? Have you made up your mind about where are you going to live for the rest of your life? Have you planned where you want to achieve or succeed?		
35	When you close your eyes can you see your life's picture? Health? Education? Finances (money)? Family relationships? Social life /friends? Assets? Religious beliefs?		
36	Are you happy when you see your own life picture?		
37	When you open your eyes, have you done something to push yourself to make you become what you want to be?		
38	When is that going to happen?		
39	Have you written it down on a piece of paper and put it under your bed? Have you completed this exercise book? Have you kept this book somewhere safe, where you can see it frequently?		
40	When should you be starting your project? The answer must be 'now'; life is too short, you must start your plans immediately.		
	Total		

REFERENCES

Adrianna Kear, Vikki Frank, Jamie Lester, Hannah Yang, (2007), <u>Centre for Higher Education Policy Analysis</u>, University of Southern California, USA.

Ann E. Smith (2009), Home is Important for People, <u>www.homelife.com</u> – accessed on 12 June 2009.

Albert Peterson (2007), The Meaning of Life, <u>International Journal of Life Development</u>, Vol. 2, No. 5, p. 12-35.

Baldauf, S.L., J.D. Palmer, and W.F. Doolittle (1996), The Root of the Universal Tree and the Origin of Eukaryotes based on Elongation Factor Phylogeny, <u>Proceedings of the Natural Academy of Sciences of the United States of America</u>, Vol. 93, p. 7749-7754.

Brown, J.R. and W.F. Doolittle (1995), Root of the Universal Tree of Life based on Ancient Aminoacy, TRNA Synthetase Gene Duplications, <u>Proceedings of the National Academy of Sciences of the United States of America</u>, Vol. 92, p. 2441-2445.

Caetano, Anolles (2002), Evolved RNA Secondary Structure and the Rooting of the Universal Tree of Life, <u>Journal of Molecular Evolution</u>, Vol. 54, p. 333-345.

Brian Tracy (2001), <u>The 21 Success Secrets of Self-Made Millionaires</u>, 235 Montgomery Street, Suite 650, San Francisco, CA 94104-2916, USA.

Brian Tracy (2004), <u>Goals: How to get everything you want faster than you ever thought possible</u>, 235 Montgomery Street, Suite 650, San Francisco, CA94104-2916, USA.

Byron Pulsifer (2007), <u>Preparation Equals Success</u>, Thoughts of Encouragement Journal, Vol. 1.

David Camphell (2008), <u>Successful in Life</u>, La Mure Ltd, France

David J. Schwartz (1959), <u>The Magic of Thinking Big</u>, Thorson Publishers Limited, Wellingborough, Northamptonshire NN8 2RQ, England, UK.

Eileen Mulligan (2000), <u>Life Coaching: Change your life in 7 days</u>, Judy Piatkus Publisher Ltd, 5 Windmill Street, London W1P 1HF, UK.

Eliyahu M. Goldratt and Jeff Cox (2000), <u>The Goal: A Process of Ongoing Improvement</u>, Second Edition, PO Box 1307, Maidenhead, Berks SL6 8JF, England, UK.

Gertrude W and Van Pelt (1998), The Ladder of Life, Life Ladder, <u>Theosophical University Press</u>, USA.

Henry David Thorea (2009), Life Skills, Module 7: Life Skills, <u>www.lifeskills.com</u> – accessed on 20 June 2009

Jessica A. Jonikas and Judith A. Cook (2004), <u>Creating Your Self-Directed Life Plan</u>, University of Illinois at Chicago, National Research and Training Centre, Chicago, USA.

John Tschohl (1999), perspectives, The Qualities of Successful People, <u>Managing Service Quality Journal</u>, Vol. 9, No. 2, pp. 88-80

Martin Van Mesdag, (2007), Intelligence and Planning, <u>International Journal Intelligence Planning</u>, Vol. 3, No. 1.

Paul Taylor (2008), Looking Backward and Forward, Pew Research Centre, <u>A Social Trends Report</u>, USA.

Petersen Jonikas (2003), <u>Self-Determination Senses; Raising Difficult Issues with Your Service Provider</u>, University of Illinois at Chicago, National Research and Training Centre, Chicago, USA.

Randy Slechta, (2008), <u>The Sixth Key to a Successful Future</u>, Leadership Management International, Lake Shore Drive, Waco, USA. Website: imi-inc.com

Shanelle Pierce (2005), <u>Four Levels of Success</u>, Centre for Life Principle, USA.

Wm. G. Seavey (2009), Straightforward life line, Lesson for Living, <u>www.thewinnerscircle.org</u> – accessed on 09 July 2009.

Victoria Tiegert (2009), Family Relationship, <u>Family Relationship Journal</u>, Vol. 12, No. 102